BACKPACKING RO

How To Books on Living & Working Abroad

Applying for a United States Visa
Backpacking Round Europe
Become an Au Pair
Doing Voluntary Work Abroad
Emigrate
Finding a Job in Canada
Finding Work Overseas
Find Temporary Work Abroad
Get a Job Abroad
Get a Job in America
Get a Job in Australia
Get a Job in Europe
Get a Job in France
Get a Job in Germany
Get a Job in Hotels & Catering
Get a Job in Travel & Tourism
Live & Work in America
Live & Work in Australia
Live & Work in France
Live & Work in Germany
Live & Work in the Gulf
Live & Work in Italy
Live & Work in Japan
Live & Work in New Zealand
Live & Work in Portugal

Living & Working in Britain
Living & Working in Canada
Living & Working in China
Living & Working in Hong Kong
Living & Working in Saudi Arabia
Living & Working in the Netherlands
Master Languages
Obtaining Visas & Work Permits
Rent & Buy Property in France
Rent & Buy Property in Italy
Retire Abroad
Selling into Japan
Setting Up Home in Florida
Spending a Year Abroad
Study Abroad
Teach Abroad
Travel Round the World
Working Abroad
Working as a Holiday Rep
Working in Japan
Working in the Gulf
Working on Contract Worldwide
Working on Cruise Ships
Your Own Business in Europe

Other titles in preparation.

The How To series now contains more than 200 titles in the following categories:

Business Basics
Family Reference
Jobs & Careers
Living and Working Abroad
Student Handbooks
Successful Writing

Please send for a free copy of the latest catalogue for full details
(see back cover for address).

TRAVEL

BACKPACKING ROUND EUROPE

How to explore Europe on a budget

Mark Hempshell

How To Books

Cartoons by Mike Flanagan

British Library Cataloguing in Publication Data
A catalogue record for this book is available from the British Library.

First published in 1997 by How To Books Ltd, 3 Newtec Place, Magdalen Road, Oxford OX4 1RE, United Kingdom. Tel: (01865) 793806. Fax: (01865) 248780.

Note: The material contained in this book is set out in good faith for general guidance and no liability can be accepted for loss or expense incurred as a result of relying in particular circumstances on statements made in the book. The laws and regulations are complex and liable to change, and readers should check the current position with the relevant authorities before making personal arrangements.

Produced for How To Books by Deer Park Productions.
Typeset by The Baskerville Press, Salisbury, Wiltshire.
Printed and bound by Cromwell Press, Broughton Gifford, Melksham, Wiltshire.

Contents

List of Illustrations

Preface

Would you like to spend a few weeks – or even a few months – exploring Europe and visiting exciting cities like Paris, Rome or Athens? Or maybe you would prefer to do something more energetic like skiing in the Alps, or even relax on a beach in the Greek Isles for a while? If you're really adventurous you might even like to venture into eastern Europe!

The truth is, you can do all this and you needn't spend thousands of pounds on expensive flights, hotels and so on. If you know where to go and what to do you can backpack for a reasonable cost – maybe as little as £20 a day.

This book tells you all you need to know to travel round Europe on a modest budget. It will tell you all you need to know to plan your trip, how to travel and stay cheaply, and even give you tips on things you can do during your stay. This book isn't a stuffy travel guide for well-heeled tourists, but neither will you have to 'rough it' all the time. It's all about having the best possible time but at the lowest possible cost. If that sounds good to you, then you'll find this book invaluable! With this book in your hand you're all set to have a great time exploring Europe. Get your map out and start planning it now!

Mark Hempshell

The countries of Europe

IS THIS YOU?

Student

Adventurous

Linguist

Fit and healthy

Free to travel

Globetrotter

Passport holder

Wanting a change

On sabbatical

Single

Wanting a challenge

Adaptable

Language student

European studies student

Taking a gap year

Keeping to a budget

Wanting a holiday

Practical

Enjoys meeting people

Likes the outdoors

Likes to experience different cultures

Enjoys walking

Ready to rough it

Would like to work abroad

Wants a break from routine

Enjoys travelling

1
Planning Your Trip

DECIDING WHERE TO GO AND WHAT TO SEE

Where to go

It is a good idea to plan some sort of itinerary before you start. It may seem tempting just to take off and go where the fancy takes you, but this is a recipe for seeing a fairly small number of places – and at a high cost too.

It is much better to have some idea of a route before you set off. It will save time and be cheaper too. This is not to say you can't change your itinerary *en route* – in fact some of the best fun is to be had this way – but you should have an overall route in mind.

Remember, Europe is a big place. It is almost 2,000 miles from Dublin to Athens and 3,000 miles from Nordkapp in Norway to Gibraltar. So, unless you have a limitless amount of time you're not going to cover every corner in just one trip.

Here are some points to bear in mind:

- *What do you like to do?* Are you interested in history, culture, general sightseeing or just having a good time?

- *How much time do you have?* This is important bearing in mind the distances involved. It takes longer to travel in some countries than others. To do everything properly don't plan to travel more than 500 miles in one week.

- *How much money do you have?* Yes, you can travel cheaply but it still costs money. If you are on a really tight budget it might be better to stick to one or two countries than try to do everything.

- *What time of year is it?* Remember that the weather in northern Europe is not always pleasant in the winter, whereas in the summer you can go more or less anywhere.

13

What to see

It can be a little unrealistic to aim to go everywhere and aim to see everything. For example, if you go to Greece for two weeks you'll be hard pushed to see all the main ancient sites and enjoy plenty of time on the beach too. It's much better to have some sort of 'theme' for your trip to make the most efficient use of your time. Try to plan your trip around those activities that you can only do in the particular country you wish to visit. For example, you can only see the Vatican if you go to Rome, but you can spend time on the beach in any country.

To help you decide what to see consider these points:

● *What are your main interests?* For example, museums, ancient sites or sporting activities and so on. Put them in order of priority.

● *How much time do you have?* Remember that some cities, like Paris, could keep you occupied for two weeks but you can see the highlights of others, like Brussels for example, in half a day.

● *How much money do you have?* Some attractions are expensive to see, whereas others are free. Most European countries offer admission to national heritage type attractions at bargain prices.

● *Are you travelling with others?* It's important that everyone should have a say in what they want to see.

Planning your itinerary

Planning your itinerary will ensure that you get the most out of your trip. You needn't plan everything down to the last minute, but you should have a general idea of where you want to be on any particular day.

Start by sitting down and making a list of all the places you would like to see. If there is more than one of you divide the time away by the number of people and each plan an itinerary for the number of days you each have. Once you have your list, get a large map of Europe. The *Daily Express Large World Map*, which also has a holiday route planning map of Europe, is very good for this purpose. You can buy it at most bookshops. Stick a map pin or drawing pin at each town or city you wish to visit.

Next, take a piece of string! Using a pen make an ink mark at each point which corresponds to 100 miles on your map. If you are using the map above the scale is 1:3,750,000 so you would make a mark every 42mm or thereabouts! If you take travelling 100 miles a day (which is actually quite optimistic, so don't exceed it) as a rough average then you can cut the length of string according to the time you have for travelling.

Now the fun begins! Put the string around all the pins in what seems to be the most direct route! Try several variations until you find the most 'economic' arrangement, *ie* the route that allows you to visit as many places as possible whilst travelling the shortest distance. This arrangement isn't foolproof since you can't easily travel between some places that seem close together on a map (for example Brest in north-western France and Penzance in Cornwall). However, it is better than just taking things at random.

Once you have put your list of destinations in the **order** you wish to visit them, look at what you are going to do in each place and how long it will take – one day, two days, seven days and so on. From this you can plan a basic itinerary comprising a list of places to visit and the time you will be spending there.

Finally, at this stage, you should start to think about how you are going to get from place to place on your route. There is lots more advice on this later in this book.

MAKING PREPARATIONS TO LEAVE

Deciding what to take
The next stage of successfully planning your trip is to decide **what you are going to take** and **what you are going to leave behind**.

There are two considerations here. Firstly, what exactly do you need? Some things you *have* to take with you because they cannot be obtained easily *en route*. However, bear in mind the weight factor. No matter how you are travelling there is going to be a lot of carrying, so your backpack has to be easy to carry. You won't be able to carry more than 15kg if you're small and 25kg if you're well-built – even less would be better.

What to take
To start you thinking here is a list of some things you will *need* to take. Remember to allow for the weight of the luggage itself.

● You will have to take your travel documents. You can't get these on the way.

- Allow for some maps, guide books *etc* (including this one!) – you might not be able to get these on the way.

- You will have to take some money, so you will need somewhere *safe* to keep it.

- You will have to take several changes of clothing. If you are going somewhere cold it will take up more weight.

- You will need some things to keep you entertained on your travels. Books and personal stereos *etc* take up quite a bit of weight.

- If you are on any medication then don't risk leaving it behind. In any case, it's a good idea to take a small first aid kit.

What to leave behind
It's just as important to make a list of things you *won't* need to take with you.

- Avoid the temptation of taking your favourite foods. It's very heavy and it's much cheaper to eat what you find along the way.

- Keep footwear to a minimum. This is heavy and the best thing is just to carry one pair – on your feet.

- Don't take expensive cameras. They are heavy and difficult to keep safe. A disposable camera is light and less likely to be stolen.

- Don't take any thick items of clothing. These are heavy and bulky too. If you are going to a cool climate layers of thin clothing are both space and heat efficient.

- Think very carefully before deciding to camp. All the equipment you will need takes up about all your space.

- Avoid taking sports equipment. It can be hired in most places.

Planning considerations
The following are eight essential points to consider when planning your trip.

1. Decide what you are really going away for. Culture? Nightlife? Work? Relaxation? If you try to do too many things it will take too long, be too rushed, involve too much tiring travelling and cost too much.

2. If you're travelling as a group do the other members share the same ideas?

3. It's much safer to travel as a group and can be cheaper too but it can be slower and involve everyone having to compromise.

4. Is there one single thing you have always wanted to see (*eg* the Parthenon in Athens?) If so do it and plan your trip around that.

5. What will wait and what won't? For example, if you want to see eastern Germany or Prague before it becomes just like the west then you'll have to move fast.

6. How do you want to travel? Do you want to jet out to your destination, or do you prefer to take things slowly, walking or cycling where possible?

7. Think about safety. Remember that the position on safety changes often. If travelling to potentially unstable locations always check the situation beforehand.

8. Finally, just how adventurous are you? Backpacking to Moscow sounds fun at the planning stage but unless you are a really adventurous, resourceful person you won't enjoy it. Consider Paris or Rome instead.

Tying up loose ends
The following is a checklist of some things which may need attending to before you go.

1. Give notice to your employer (including any part-time jobs).

2. Book your travel tickets for journeys where it is cheaper to book well ahead.

3. If you are going on to college, confirm start dates.

4. If you are taking a year off confirm your course for next year.

5. If you are waiting for exam results arrange for someone to collect or forward them for you.

6. Arrange for someone at home to deal with any urgent matters or emergencies for you.

7. Make a list of emergency contact numbers at home – and in each country you are visiting – and put it in a safe place.

8. Leave your itinerary with someone at home.

9. Just before leaving, confirm flight/train/bus departure times in case they have changed.

10. Book your first night's accommodation before leaving – you'll be glad you did when you arrive.

MONEY-SAVING TIPS

Managing on £20 a day

You might not believe it, but you can backpack quite happily on **£20 a day** – or less. It needs careful planning of course, but if your budget is really tight it is possible.

When you think about what that means over the course of a two week trip – as little as £280 – this represents amazing value. Yes, you can get a package holiday in the sun for that much but you'll have all sorts of extra expenses on top and you won't see anything like as much as when you backpack.

To stay within this budget you will need to plan very well. Firstly, don't be unrealistic about the distance. Three or four countries is probably a maximum on such a budget and long hauls like the UK to the Greek islands are probably not a good idea. Also choose your actual countries with care. Expensive countries like Switzerland, Austria and most of Scandinavia are off-limits and even Germany can be expensive. Spain, Portugal and even France and Italy (away from the most expensive cities) are more realistic destinations if you are trying to keep to a tight budget.

Budgeting tips
Here are some **tips** that will help you get by on £20 a day:

- Plan your route so as to avoid having to change it. Changes can work out expensive.

- Have a daily budget (£20 or whatever) and stick to it. To make this easier know approximately how much £20 is in the currency of the country you are visiting.

- Make a note of what you spend so you can stick to your budget. Don't be tempted to borrow from one day so that you can overspend on another.

- Look for 'honeypots'. They may be a bit touristy but you can do lots of different things without spending a lot on travel. For example, in Athens you can enjoy the culture, spend a day on the beach at Glyfada and share Greek village life by taking a short 30 minute bus trip out of the city.

- Don't plan to travel every day. It eats into your budget more than almost anything else.

- Make use of cheap or free accommodation, such as sleeping on coaches or trains. Also consider camping (although remember that the tent *etc* will take up most of your luggage space).

- Have one large meal a day rather than lots of snacks – these are overpriced in almost every country.

- Look for free entertainment, such as ancient sites rather than museums and music bars rather than nightclubs.

- Travel in good weather wherever possible. It *always* works out cheaper in terms of food, clothes and entertainment.

- Travel early or late. There are more cheap travel and accommodation bargains to be had May–June and in September than in July and August.

- Pay for what you can before you go. It is not as easy to overspend.

- Consider taking a credit card. If you are visiting several countries you won't have to keep paying out to change one type of foreign currency into another and so on. If you're worried about running up a large debt put your money into the account before you go.

- When changing money, change everyone's cash together as this will mean you only pay one transaction charge and you may even get a higher exchange rate for larger sums.

- If you're going as a group share things which you don't need one each of, such as a camera. This way you'll have more space to carry things that you won't have to buy on the way, such as food.

- Avoid staying in popular tourist towns, cities and resorts which are always overpriced. Instead, base yourself a few miles away and travel in by bus. You'll save a small fortune.

- Buy your travel tickets, excursions and entry tickets where the locals buy them (ask!) rather than at smart travel agencies and tourist offices where tourists tend to shop.

- Buy food, drink and gifts in back street shops which are usually much cheaper. Try telling the shopkeeper you are living in his/her town for a few months as shops in some resorts operate a dual pricing system for residents and tourists.

- If you're travelling as a group look for hotels, hostels and campsites which charge per room (or per tent) rather than per person as this will work out much cheaper.

- Look for activities and entertainments aimed at students which are almost always cut-priced. There is nothing to say you have to be a student in that country. In many places you don't even have to be a student to claim a student discount if you just ask for it!

- Avoid anything aimed at tourists as it is usually overpriced.

- Talk to your fellow travellers. People who have been in your chosen destination for a few days or weeks will know about all the best deals and cheapest places to go.

2
Getting Cut-Price Travel

There is little doubt that the cost of travel will be your biggest expense. So, this is where you can make the biggest savings on your backpacking trip.

You might think that you know about the main ways of travelling cheaply – walking, hitching, taking the bus or so on. But did you know how much you can save simply by making sure you buy the *right* ticket – and buying it in the *right* place? In some cases you will pay 300 per cent more by buying the same travel ticket from the most expensive source rather than the cheapest.

In this section we will look at all the methods of travel you might consider. *Don't* concentrate just on what *seem* cheap ways of travel (such as bus) and avoid what *seem* to be expensive ones (such as air) as this is not always the case.

TRAVELLING CHEAPLY

Getting cheap air travel

Don't ignore air travel because you assume it's expensive. Mile for mile it is often cheaper than even the local bus! Although you probably won't want to spend all your trip jetting around it can be a good idea if you want to get out to a far-flung area quickly. Why not travel out by air and travel back at your leisure by land?

To get the cheapest air travel always book with care. Never telephone the airline or walk into your local travel agent to make a booking. Go to a discount air ticket outlet. You will see lots of these advertising in the Sunday newspapers. As long as you obtain your ticket when you pay for it, and your travel is with an IATA (International Air Transport Association) member airline, you will not lose your money if either the agent or the airline (or both) fail.

Always travel off peak. There is a huge difference between travelling at peak times (when business people want to travel) and off peak. The cheapest flights are usually during the night.

Next, **always ask for a discount**. This is ideal if you are a student or under 25. Also just asking for a discount can be enough to encourage the agent to 'invent' one just to make the sale – but you do have to ask.

If you can, consider an unusual route. Journeys which involve stopovers and round-about trips can often be much cheaper than direct flights as airlines price more keenly on these routes.

Finally, always check to see if a seat is available on a **charter flight**. These are aimed at holiday-makers and so are usually considerably cheaper than scheduled flights which are aimed at business travellers. In theory, with a charter flight, you normally have to book several weeks in advance but some agents are able to backdate tickets to make charter travel as convenient as scheduled travel.

Getting cheap rail travel

Train travel is certainly one of the nicest ways of travelling as you get to see the sights and meet the people. It is cheap, because it's heavily subsidised in most European countries, and also incredibly reliable – especially in Scandinavia, Germany and Switzerland.

The best way of getting cheap rail travel is to book in advance when possible, preferably before leaving home. It is almost always cheaper this way than simply turning up at the station. Many national railway companies have a tourist or discount pass which works out much cheaper than buying individual tickets. Some of these are obscure, so always ask around at the planning stage of your trip.

Always use special tickets, such as Inter Rail or Eurorail. These are normally incredible bargains – *but* only if you plan to do a lot of travelling by rail. They are not recommended if you plan to take just a single journey.

In most countries non-express or stopping trains are usually much cheaper (plus you get to see a lot more of the countryside). Express trains sometimes carry a steep supplement. As with air travel, always choose less popular routes. Routes from major city to major city are often more expensive since they are heavily used by business travellers. You can often get a much cheaper ticket by travelling to a nearby town and then taking the bus, or even by travelling out from a suburban station rather than the city centre. You can also discover some nice out-of-the-way spots this way too!

Getting cheap road travel

Road travel can be a pleasant way of travelling in that it lets you see plenty of the country. However, even on express coach services, long journeys can take a long time due to poor roads, congestion or just drivers who are in no great rush to get to their destination. When considering a coach trip think realistically about how long it is going to take.

With road travel, you should travel last minute for the best bargains. Unless that is, you really want to travel a particular route at a particular time. You can often get bargains, especially at foreign bus stations, where many operators compete for your business and there is rarely a shortage of seats.

Always go for a return ticket. This usually works out much cheaper than a single ticket if you are likely to use the return. (If you do not use the return you may be able to sell it to other travellers once you reach your destination). Again, **always shop around**. There is stiff competition in most countries and you may find a big difference between the nationally-owned coach company and private operators. The newest coaches will also be dearer. Although the advantage is that they offer a better degree of safety.

Non-express or stopping coaches are usually much cheaper, plus you get to see even more of the countryside. Express coaches and 'executive' services often carry a supplement.

Finally, as always, ask for a discount. Most operators give discounts to students and if they are small, private operators you can get a discount even if you are not a student or don't have the appropriate identification.

TRAVELLING FREE

Hitchhiking safely and successfully
Hitchhiking can be an excellent way of travelling as it is free (or almost free), often quite comfortable, and you also get to mix with the local people. On the minus side, of course, it can be quite unreliable and also dangerous in some places.

Before hitchhiking for all or part of your trip always do your homework. Find out if hitchhiking is (a) possible and (b) safe. Women should note that it is usually *easier* for them to get lifts but not always *safe*, certainly not if alone, and possibly not even if travelling in pairs.

Always plan your route. Hitchhiking may be a casual way of travelling but you will do better if you know where you want to go and where you can get lifts. It is always important to stand where drivers can stop. Remember stopping on motorways and equivalent high-speed roads is illegal in almost every European country. Plan your trip so that one lift will end where it will be easy to get another, *ie* at a service area rather than a motorway junction.

It always pays to look clean and respectable and dress as smartly as your circumstances allow. Lorry drivers might not mind picking up a scruffily dressed backpacker but it will certainly reduce the number of lifts you get in cars!

Finally, **always put safety first**. If you are in any doubts about the motives of the driver always demand that they stop and get out immediately.

Organised hitchhiking

Hitchhiking need not be a haphazard business. In some countries there are hitchhiking clubs. These clubs charge a small fee but will match you up with any drivers who are also members of the club and who are going your way.

You can often find out about these clubs from tourist offices. See Figure 1 for a list of some of the main ones together with their telephone numbers.

BELGIUM

Taxistop

Brussels: 02 511 6930   Liege: 041 323870

FRANCE

Allostop-Provoya

Lille: 20 57 96 69   Paris: 1 246 0066

Strasbourg:88 37 13 13   Toulouse: 61 22 68 13

GERMANY

Mitfahrzentrale

Munich: 89 594561

UNITED KINGDOM

The Backpacker's Club: PO Box 381, Reading RG3 4RL.

Fig. 1. Examples of hitchhiking clubs.

Biking your way round Europe

It is worth considering biking if you are a keen cyclist and also reasonably fit. The main advantage is that it is cheap and maintenance is easy in most countries. You will, however, be even more restricted in what you can take than if you are just backpacking.

If you are thinking about biking check out the situation before leaving. Some countries are very pro-cycling, especially France and the Netherlands. Spain, Italy and Germany are also quite cyclist-friendly. They offer good roads and even special cycle tracks. Hostels and hotels usually have somewhere to store your bike. In countries such as Greece or Portugal, on the other hand, roads can be poor and special provision for cyclists unknown.

The cheapest method is to take your own bike. However, if you don't want to cycle all the way you could consider renting a bike for part of the journey. This is possible in many places, including at most railway stations in France and the Netherlands and some other countries. If you are planning a longer stay then buying a secondhand bike when you arrive and selling it before you come home can work out less expensive.

Tips for cyclists

Here are some more tips for cyclists:

- Plan your route carefully before you go. Don't attempt more than 30 miles per day unless you are an experienced cyclist.

- Plan your route around railway lines and stations. If you want a break from cycling it's easy to transport your bike by train, but not so easy by air or coach!

- Always take a map which is detailed enough to show cycle tracks and side roads. This should be a minimum scale of 1:25,000, otherwise you'll find yourself planning a journey that involves too many main roads.

- There is usually no need to take a lot of spares. In the pro-cycling countries almost every village has a bike shop and if they don't have the spare you need they will improvise something.

- Be sure to get insured, as there is a higher risk of being involved in an accident or suffering theft when cycling.

● There should be no customs problems in most of western Europe. If travelling to eastern Europe you should check what restrictions there are on temporarily importing a cycle.

● If you're not an experienced cyclist then **train, train** and **train** again until you can easily cope with long distances.

Exploring other ways of travelling cheaply
Travelling inexpensively involves using your imagination. Here are five ways you can travel cheaply which you might not have thought about:

Hiring a car
Hiring a car is likely to be prohibitively expensive if you are travelling alone, or in a pair, but if there are three, four or five of you to share the cost it can work out much cheaper than public transport, *ie* as little as £50 per week off-season in Spain or Portugal.

Buying a car
This may be a possibility worth thinking about if you are planning a longer trip and know a little about cars. If you buy something old and cheap there is every chance you will be able to resell it for almost as much a few weeks later. If you do this be sure to take out motor insurance as well as ordinary travel insurance as often this does not cover you for medical treatment if you suffer an accident whilst driving or travelling in a motor vehicle.

Working as an air courier
This is ideal for backpackers as you are allowed to take cabin baggage (a medium-sized backpack will fit the cabin baggage limits of most airlines) but not hold luggage. If you are interested in this contact one of the many courier companies for details. Contrary to what you might have heard air courier travel is rarely free. You usually have to pay something on most routes. (In some cases this may not be much less than a discount ticket.) Also, if you are travelling in a group it can be difficult to get three or four courier tickets on the same flight.
    Air courier companies in the UK include: Bridges Worldwide (Tel: (0181) 759 5050), CTS (Tel: (0171) 351 0300) and Jupiter (Tel: (01753) 689989).

Sharing expenses
If you are starting your trip with a fairly long journey then it can be

worth placing an advertisement in your local paper, stating your destination, and offering to share expenses with a car or lorry driver who is going the same way. This could lead to a door-to-door trip at a considerable saving.

Using package holidays
Always investigate the cost of an air, rail or coach package holiday to your chosen destination before a travel-only ticket. You might find that it is actually cheaper to buy an inclusive package tour than just a flight since these holidays make use of group booking rates. For example, there are off-peak deals to Spain or Greece for £99 most years and you get a week's accommodation too. There is nothing to say you have to use the accommodation or the return transport.

Travelling free
You might not believe it, but it is possible to get **free travel!** These methods do involve a degree of imagination and determination but, when you consider you could save hundreds of pounds – just for a little cheek – they are certainly worth following up. Here are five ideas for getting free travel:

Tour escort work
Some land package companies need guides to escort their coach or rail tours. If you are presentable and mature and have experience of working with people (even if only in a part-time job) you might be able to get a temporary job or a one-off journey. Look at the advertisements for this type of work in the *Overseas Jobs Express* newspaper.

Car delivery
Another free travel possibility is to offer to drive a car to someone's holiday home, in perhaps Spain or Italy. You would not normally expect to be paid but you would expect your customer to pay for all insurance, petrol and road tolls. Place an advertisement in your local paper in advance of the summer season.

Driving jobs
Some haulage and long distance removal companies hire drivers on temporary or one-off contracts to deliver loads across Europe. If you can't drive then you might be employed as a driver's mate to help with loading and unloading. A quick 'phone call to all haulage and

removals companies in the local *Yellow Pages* may turn up some possibilities. Whilst you would normally expect to be paid, an offer to do the job free in return for travel could prove very tempting to these companies.

Travel writing
If you have a flair for writing offer an article or report on your chosen destinations to newspapers and magazines who cover travel subjects. Then approach companies who run holidays to your chosen destination, airlines, hoteliers and so on offering to include them in your article or review in exchange for free travel or accommodation. A letter of introduction from a well known newspaper or magazine can open many doors that would otherwise remain closed!

Yacht crewing
Privately owned and charter yachts and barges frequently take on deck hands to help with cooking, cleaning and general maintenance. This work is often badly paid or even unpaid but you do receive free travel and accommodation. Such jobs can be found by reading the yachting and boating press and asking round at marinas. A book called *How to Get Work on Luxury Yachts and Superyachts* (Harp Publications) also explains how to get this work.

Useful tip: Remember that you can take advantage of these cheap and free methods of travel once you are out and about backpacking around Europe. They do not always have to be planned before leaving home and, in fact, it is easier to find out about them once you are on the road.

USEFUL SOURCES FOR CHEAP TRAVEL

Finding bargain priced tickets
Here are some companies who specialise in supplying all types of travel tickets at the keenest possible prices. They are also well established, so offer a degree of protection for your money:

Campus Travel
Has 36 branches around the UK. The main one is at 52 Grosvenor Gardens, London SW1W 0AG. Tel: (0171) 730 3402.

Council Travel
Has offices around Europe. The UK office is at 28a Poland Street, London W1V 3DB. Tel: (0171) 287 3337.

STA
Has branches around the UK. Head office is Priory House, 6 Wrights Lane, London W8 6TA. Tel: (0171) 938 4711.

Trailfinders
Has branches around the UK. Head office is 42/50 Earls Court Road, London W8 6EJ. Tel: (0171) 938 3366.

WEXAS International
Is based at 45–49 Brompton Road, London SW3 1DE. Tel: (0171) 589 3315.

Getting travel discount cards and passes
Discount cards
It is always worth looking at what discount cards you can take advantage of before you travel. These can be used to get money off food, hotels and hostels, travel, entertainment and general shopping and the discounts they offer can range between 5 per cent and as much as 50 per cent depending on the country and what you are buying.

There are two main cards which offer discounts throughout Europe (and also worldwide) to both students and non-students. These charge a subscription fee but they also come with a handbook of organisations which offer discounts to the holder.

- **ISIC (International Student Identity Card).** This is available to students from their local students travel office or from ISIC Mail Order, Bleaklow House, Mill Street, Glossop, Derbyshire SK13 8PT.

- **IYIDC (International Youth ID Card).** This is available to everyone under 26, not just students, and offers over 11,000 discount goods and services worldwide. This is available from FIYTO, 81 Islands Brygge, 2300 Copenhagen S. Denmark and several youth agencies worldwide including London Student Travel, 52 Grosvenor Gardens, London SW1W 0AG. (In the USA: CIEE, 205 East 42nd Street, New York, NY10017).

Finally, if you are a student then be sure to take your ID card from your school, college or university. It is always worth producing it when you go into a shop, travel agency or hotel and asking if there is a student discount. Traders won't volunteer a discount unless you ask!

Passes
The following is a list of available passes for Europe as a whole:

- **Billet International Pour Jeune**. Reduced bus and train fares for those up to 26 years old. It is valid for 60 days.

- **Eurail Pass**. There are a variety of passes. Ask your travel agent for details. Of particular use is the Eurail Youth Pass for groups of three or more travellers under 26 and the Eurail Saver pass which is similar but offers first-class travel.

- **Inter Rail Pass**. The famous Inter Rail pass allows one month's unlimited rail travel in most of Europe, for under 26s only. More information is given about this later in the book.

There are also passes for individual countries:

Austria
- *National pass*: valid for one month's unlimited rail travel within Austria.

- *Puzzle ticket*: valid for trains and buses on any 4 days out of 10 days. You can get a ticket for each of four zones within the country.

Belgium
- *Benelux Five Day Rail Pass*: offers unlimited travel throughout Belgium, Netherlands and Luxembourg.

- *Roundabout Ticket*: offers unlimited rail and some bus travel throughout Belgium. Tickets are available for different lengths of stay.

Denmark
- *Scanrail Pass*: this allows 21 days unlimited travel in all the Scandinavian countries (Denmark, Norway, Sweden, Finland).

France
● *French Rail Pass*: offers unlimited travel for nine days within the month. A pass allowing four days travel within 15 days is also available.

Germany
● Bodensee Pass: unlimited rail and some bus travel for the under 23s (under 26 if a student).

Ireland
● *Rambler and Overlander Rail Passes* are available.

Italy
● *Travel at Will Card*: available in UK only, it offers unlimited rail travel for one month.

Luxembourg
● *Benelux Five Day Rail Pass*: offers unlimited travel throughout Belgium, Netherlands and Luxembourg.

Netherlands
● *Benelux Five Day Rail Pass*: offers unlimited travel throughout Belgium, Netherlands and Luxembourg.

Poland
● *PoleRail Pass*: offers unlimited travel for a period of either 7, 14 or 21 days.

Switzerland
● Swiss Pass: one month's unlimited rail travel. Also offers travel on some post buses and some lake ferries.

United Kingdom
(Available to visitors from abroad only).

● *BritExpress Card*: 30 per cent off rail travel for a 30 day period.

● *Tourist Trail Pass*: unlimited rail travel for up to 30 days.

Travel agents and tourist offices can supply these passes, or tell you where to obtain them.

GETTING THE BEST FROM AN INTER RAIL TICKET

The **Inter Rail pass** is still one of Europe's great travel bargains and well worth considering for backpackers and, indeed, all young people travelling on a budget. You can travel long distances for what works out at only pennies per kilometre.

However, the Inter Rail ticket does have its drawbacks. Once you have your ticket you will be tempted to take incredibly long journeys in order to get your money's worth. This can prove boring and also quite time consuming! Plus you will also find that whereas it is easy to make journeys on major routes it is quite difficult to plan rail travel on local lines until you actually arrive in the country.

Finding out who is eligible

To get an Inter Rail pass you must be under 26 years old. You must buy it in your country of residence, having been resident there for at least six months.

If you are 26 or over you can get an Inter Rail Plus pass or a Eurail pass which is not quite as good value but still a reasonably-priced way of travelling by rail. Your travel agent will tell you where to obtain your Inter Rail pass.

Where can you travel?

Passes are available on a **zone basis**. A full Inter Rail pass is valid for travel in every western European country plus the Czech Republic, Hungary and Romania. You can also travel in Morocco and Turkey (even the Asian part) at no extra cost. It doesn't provide free travel in the country in which you purchase the pass, although it does offer a discount.

For a supplement you can extend your Inter Rail pass to cover ferry crossings across the Mediterranean, Irish Sea and Baltic Sea. It doesn't cover the English Channel, however, so it is only worth taking this option if you are sure you wish to make use of the crossings it does cover.

Planning your trip

If you buy an Inter Rail pass it is very important to plan your journey carefully to get maximum value from it. Also take care not to overstretch yourself so that onward travel connections cost you more than you save. For example, you can get from Ireland to Greece and back in a month – sightseeing as you go – but only just!

You will need a good timetable to plan your trip properly, and should also take it with you. Thomas Cook's *Continental European Timetable* is the best timetable for this purpose and is available at most large bookshops. It doesn't cover the smaller local routes, however – you can only find out about these once you are actually in the country yourself.

Although your Inter Rail pass offers you unlimited travel try and plan the shortest journeys possible that allow you to see all you wish to see. Also try to plan a circular route rather than an outward and return trip on the same line. That extra journey might be 'free' but it is still very time-consuming and one side of the railway track looks very much like the other!

Making a success of your trip

One of the advantages of Inter Rail travel is that, as you are travelling mostly by train, luggage is less of a problem. There is plenty of room on most trains and there are lockers and left-luggage offices at the main line stations in most countries. This is ideal for the inter-railer who sightsees by day and uses the train as a 'travelling hotel' overnight. If you take a small day-pack as well as your backpack you can leave most of your luggage at the station and travel around unencumbered during the day!

Do take some books and a personal hi-fi *etc* as many journeys are through industrial areas rather than attractive scenery.

Where possible buy food away from the station and take it with you. Food is expensive in most trains and stations and not always of very good quality – plus if you get off to buy food and drink you could easily miss the train!

Finally, always take security seriously. Robbers operate on some trains and there are also petty thieves in most countries. It is a good idea to lock your luggage to some immovable object and keep money and important documents in a money belt. This is particularly important if you wish to sleep on the train – although it's a good way of saving on accommodation costs it can be risky.

Suggested routes

The great thing about Inter Rail travel is that you can go where you please without having to ask about the fare. However, some interesting journeys you might like to consider are:

● *Paris to the South of France*: A classic train journey where northern Europe gradually changes into a Mediterranean atmosphere.

- *Trans-Italy*: A chance to see the many faces of this country, especially the contrast between the north and south.

- *Sweden*: Rail is the very best way to see this country quickly.

- *Switzerland and Austria*: Probably the cheapest way you will find of visiting these (normally very expensive) countries.

- *London to Athens:* One of Europe's longest train journeys providing so many contrasts (but also quite boring in places!).

Do's and don'ts of Inter Railing

Do be realistic about how far you can go. Unless you're a train lover it can get boring after a while.

Do think about how you'll return, before setting off on the next leg.

Do plan several overnight train journeys where possible. This saves the cost of a hotel.

Do ring ahead and book your accommodation if you're arriving in a strange place late at night.

Do make sure your pass is valid for the train you use. It doesn't cover some express trains (such as the French TGV), private railways, funiculars, underground systems and tourist-attraction type lines.

Don't buy an Inter Rail pass if you mainly want to visit just one country.

Don't be tempted to go too far to get your money's worth!

Don't rely on the timetable totally. Even in the most organised countries things can go wrong and mistakes can be made. Double-check with the booking office.

Don't accidentally miss the expiry date unless you know what it will cost to return home at full fare price.

3
Getting Cut-Price Accommodation

FINDING ACCOMMODATION

In this section we will look at how to get the best bargains in **accommodation**, whether you want to stay in hotels, hostels or guest houses – and even explain how you can stay overnight for absolutely no cost whatsoever!

Getting discount on any hotel

The term **hotel** covers a very wide range of accommodation from luxurious five-star establishments, to rooms above pubs and bars. Even if you are on a tight budget never think that you won't be able to afford a hotel. Hotels in some countries are cheaper than in others and, by booking your room carefully, you can often save a small fortune on what is known as the **rack rate** (the advertised nightly charge).

First of all, avoid booking in advance if possible. The best rates are usually to be had on the spot, by shopping around. If you want the peace of mind of booking your next night's accommodation in advance then only book for one night and then check local rates once you arrive.

Again, always do your homework. Tourist guides often include lists of hotels and many tourist offices will supply a free list on request. Once you arrive you can then 'phone or visit suitable hotels, rather than waste time walking the streets.

Tips for getting cheaper rates
The following are some tips for obtaining **discounted rates**:

● Always *ask* for a discount! This is the norm in many countries but can still work even where it isn't.

- *Never* pay the **rack rate**. Telephone first if you find face-to-face bargaining difficult. (Many hotels have a freephone number.)

- Avoid booking through national booking centres.

- Avoid booking through airport and railway stands and tourist offices.

- Note that some hotels and hotel chains (such as *Formule 1* in France) charge per room not per person. Sharing can reduce the cost to only a small amount each.

- Make use of discount cards and frequent-user passes where available.

- Ask if there is a price without breakfast which is usually much cheaper than just the cost of the food.

Using and choosing youth hostels

You will find youth hostels exist in all European countries. However, the picture varies across Europe. There are plenty in most of western Europe, although they are less numerous in France and Italy. There are plenty in Poland, the Czech Republic, Hungary and Bulgaria, though few elsewhere in this part of the continent. The tourist office of each country can normally supply a list of youth hostels in the area.

The International Youth Hostel Federation (IYHF) has 5000 hostels worldwide. Hostels can normally be used by non-members but it makes sense to join your relevant national youth hostel association (YHA) as the membership is usually very little and non-members are frequently charged more per night. All the hostels you can use are listed in their *Guide to Budget Accommodation* which can be bought at most bookshops.

In the United Kingdom the relevant IYHF addresses are:

Scottish Youth Hostels Association, 7 Glebe Crescent, Stirling FK8 2JA. Tel: (01786) 51181.

Youth Hostels Association (England and Wales), 8 St Stephen's Hill, St Albans, Herts AL1 2DY. Tel: (01727) 55215.

IYHF hostels can usually be used by people of all ages though those

under 26 get priority at busy times. Also at busy times your stay may
be restricted, often to three nights.

Lodging in private houses

Lodging in private houses is usually quite cheap, with the added
advantage that you get to stay a while as part of the local community
too.

Although private rooms are available in most countries you will find
a very good selection in Greece and also in most parts of eastern
Europe where many people rent out rooms to supplement their
income.

The main difficulty with lodging in private houses is that it is
difficult to find out about them in advance. You should ask the tourist
offices of the countries you wish to visit if they have any lists. If they
don't, the only option is to wait until you arrive and then go in search
of suitable lodgings. It helps to try and find out, and remember, the
local term for **Bed and Breakfast** (for example, in Germany, look for
Zimmer Frei or **Fremdenzimmer**).

Camping – what you need

Camping is worth considering because it provides cheap
accommodation. However, its main limitations are that it takes up
most of your luggage and is only really suitable for Europe (including
Mediterranean countries) in summer.

There are plenty of campsites in every European country and their
quality varies as do their prices. You can obtain details of sites from
tour guides and tourist offices.

In the height of summer sites often need to be booked in advance.
For example, in the south of France it is almost impossible to find a
modestly-priced site in July and August.

Although local laws vary it is either illegal or frowned upon to camp
rough in any country without the landowner's permission. The main
exception to this is most of Scandinavia where it is a legal right!
Farmers will often give you permission but, in most places, camping on
the beach will frequently attract the attention of the local police.

Some campsites expect you to have a **camping carnet** although,
strictly, it is not a legal requirement in any country. This provides
insurance for your equipment and also serves as a form of ID (some
campsites will, otherwise, expect to keep your passport during your
stay). In the UK you can obtain a camping carnet from the Camping
and Caravanning Club, Green Fields House, Westwood Way, Coventry
CV4 8SH. Tel: (01203) 694995.

Other sources of inexpensive accommodation

Here are some other ways you can find a place to stay on your travels
for very little money:

● **Caravan parks**: Some places, especially France and Spain, have
residential caravan sites where you can stay. These are very cheap
early and late in the season. Ask the tourist office.

● **Live-in accommodation**: If you are willing to do a few days' work
here and there you could get a job (for example, in a hotel) that
provides accommodation.

● **Universities and colleges**: Many rent out their halls of residence
during vacations. Just ask on the local campus.

● **Temporary summer accommodation**: In some countries youth
organisations set up temporary summer dormitories to cater for the
influx of summer visitors. This accommodation will probably only
be basic, such as in a community hall or gym, but it will be very
cheap. Ask the local tourist office.

● **Pubs and bars**: These sometimes rent out rooms but it is necessary
to ask, as they do not always advertise.

● **Overnight trains**: These offer a very cheap place to stay, although
they can be uncomfortable and risky from a security point of view.
Think twice about paying out for a sleeping berth as it can work out
more costly than a modest hotel room.

FINDING FREE ACCOMMODATION

Five ways to get free accommodation

It is possible to get **free accommodation** during your travels. Of course,
this may be quite basic and really only for the more adventurous
backpacker. However, a few nights in this free accommodation could
save you a great deal of money, as well as being an interesting
experience!

Here are some ways to enjoy free accommodation:

1. **Farmer's barns and outbuildings**: A realistic possibility in summer.
Some farmers are willing to give you permission to do this,
especially in quieter country areas where not much else is available.

2. **Charity hostels**: These are always a possibility if you are stuck, especially in cities. You might, however, be expected to attend a religious service or undergo some kind of 'counselling'.

3. **Churches**: Churches in some areas allow needy travellers to stay on their premises, or in church halls and so on. Ask for the local clergyman.

4. **Private homes**: It is sometimes possible to stay in private homes free by getting to know people in pubs, bars and so on. This is more likely in rural areas where people are usually more hospitable. Obviously this needs to be done with care, especially if you are a lone traveller.

5. **Sleeping rough**: This is an option that many backpackers consider from time to time. Choose your location with care, making sure that your chosen spot is as safe as possible. Sleeping rough is either illegal or frowned upon in most places and sleeping in public parks or on beaches often attracts police attention very quickly. Airports, railway stations and bus stations are possibilities and you're unlikely to be turned away if you have a ticket for onward travel.

You will find details of organisations which can help young people find and arrange budget priced accommodation and travel in Chapter 6 under the 'Travel tips' and 'Accommodation tips' headings.

4
The A–Z of Backpacking

In this section we will provide you with all the day-to-day information you will need for your trip. If you read up on it before you go, and also keep it handy throughout your travels, you should find that you have whatever information you need no matter what situation you find yourself in.

COMMUNICATING

Making 'phone calls
Remember to make a note of all the telephone numbers you are likely to want to call, both at home and abroad, before leaving. It may be impossible to find them once you are abroad.

Despite some harmonisation the telephone systems operate in a totally different way in every European country. The main difference are as follows:

● In some countries not all 'phones can make international calls. In some places you must go to the post office or a call office to do this.

● In remote locations where there are no call boxes you can use payphones in shops and bars. You do not have to be a customer.

● Not all public 'phones take coins. 'Phone cards are more usual in most countries. You can usually buy these from a local shop or kiosk.

See Figure 2 for a list of some useful international dialling codes.

When dialling **to** the country in question dial the code shown in the first column **after** the dial-out code of the country you are calling **from** (the number in the second column) but before the subscriber's number.

Country	Dial-to code	Dial-out code
Albania	355	N/A*
Austria	43	00
Baltic States		
Estonia	372	00
Latvia	371	00
Lithuania	370	00
Belarus	375	00
Belgium	32	00
Bulgaria	359	00
Czech Republic	42	00
Denmark	45	00
Finland	358	00
France	33	00
Germany	49	00
Greece	30	00
Hungary	36	00
Ireland	353	00
Italy	39	00
Luxembourg	352	00
Netherlands	31	00
Norway	47	00
Poland	48	00
Portugal	351	00
Romania	40	00
Russia	7	00
Slovak Republic	42	00
Spain	34	00
Sweden	46	00
Switzerland	41	00
Ukraine	380	00
United Kingdom	44	00

* Up-to-date information not available at time of writing.

Fig. 2. International dialling codes.

When dialling **out** of the country in question dial the code shown in the second column **before** the dial-in code of the country you wish to call **followed** by the subscriber's number.

Using the post offices in Europe
In most European countries the post office serves as an important centre of communications. Not only can you send letters and parcels there, but you can usually send telegrams and make telephone calls. Many European post offices also offer giro banking facilities so you can cash travellers cheques, or draw money on a credit card.

Here are some tips that will help you at the post office:

● Different windows may be dedicated to different services. Check before joining a long queue!

● Many countries do not have sub-post offices. In some areas local shops act as an agency instead.

● Post offices in many places are reluctant to sell stamps only! Buy your stamps from a shop or kiosk instead.

● Post office hours vary from office to office. In most large European cities there will be a main post office open late during the working week.

● You can have mail sent to you *post restante* or *care of* the local post office in many countries. When you go to collect it, take your passport as ID. (If you have American Express travellers cheques you can have mail sent to you care of the local American Express office. These are found in most large European cities.)

UNDERSTANDING CUSTOMS

Customs allowances in Europe
Customs regulations are one aspect that can cause problems for travellers. However, in recent years much has been done to simplify customs regulations between the European Union (EU) countries.

When crossing land borders between EU countries by road or rail you are unlikely to be stopped as a matter of course, but routine customs checks are carried out from time to time. At sea and airports many countries operate a red, green and blue channel system:

- The blue channel is for passengers travelling from other EU countries.

- The green channel is for those from non-EU countries with nothing to declare.

- The red channel is for those with dutiable or restricted goods they wish to declare to customs.

No matter where you are travelling from there are limits on the amount of goods you may import which have been purchased in a duty-free rather than a duty-paid shop. Figure 3 shows what these are at the time of writing.

Remember that apart from the usual duty-free tobacco and alcohol allowances other items are banned or restricted from import into most countries. These are mainly:

- controlled drugs

- pornography

- firearms and dangerous weapons

- counterfeit and fake goods

- imports of money (cash) may be limited in some countries.

Dealing with problems at customs
It is worth remembering that, unfortunately, backpackers often attract extra attention from customs and may be subject to more random checks than other travellers. As such, the following advice may be helpful:

- Double-check your duty-free allowances before leaving your previous stop.

- If in doubt declare goods which you think might be restricted or over duty-free limits.

- Remember that there are sometimes different customs allowances based on your country of residence and not just which country you are arriving from.

Duty-free allowances in Europe

Albania	Reasonable amount of alcohol and tobacco for personal use.
Austria	200 cigarettes/50 cigars/250g tobacco/1 litre spirits/2 litres wine

Baltic States
  Estonia
  Latvia
  Lithuania
	
	N/A
	N/A
	N/A

Belarus	N/A
Belgium	50g perfume/1 litre spirits/2 litres wine
Bulgaria	1 litre spirits/2 litres wine/250g tobacco/100g perfume/100 BGL gifts
Czech Republic	1 litre spirits/2 litres wine/500g perfume/250 cigarettes/500 CSK gifts
Denmark	200 cigarettes/50 cigars/200g tobacco/1 litre spirits/2 litres wine/DKK 3,100 gifts
Finland *	200 cigarettes/250g tobacco/2 litres beer/1 litre wine
France *	200 cigarettes/50 cigars/250g tobacco/50g perfume/1 litre spirits/300F gifts
Germany *	200 cigarettes/50 cigars/250g tobacco/1 litre spirits/2 litres wine/50g perfume/DM 115 gifts
Greece *	200 cigarettes/50 cigars/250g tobacco/1 litre spirits/2 litres wine/50g perfume/Dr 7000 gifts
Hungary	250 cigarettes/50 cigars/250g tobacco/2 litres wine/1 litre spirits/200g perfume/F 5000 gifts
Ireland *	200 cigarettes/50 cigars/250g tobacco/1 litre spirits/2 litres wine/50g perfume/IR£34 gifts
Italy *	400 cigarettes/100 cigars/500g tobacco/0.75 litre spirits/50g perfume/500g coffee/100g tea/67,000 lire gifts

Fig. 3. Chart showing duty-free allowances in Europe

Luxembourg *	200 cigarettes/50 cigars/250g tobacco/1 litre spirits/2 litres wine/50g perfume/LF 2000 gifts
Netherlands *	200 cigarettes/50 cigars/250g tobacco/1 litre spirits/2 litres wine/50g perfume/125 Guilders gifts (8 litres of wine if from Luxembourg).
Norway	From Europe: 200 cigarettes/250g tobacco/200 cig. papers/1 litre spirits/1 litre wine/2 litres beer/1200 Kroner gifts. From elsewhere: cigarette and tobacco allowance double Europe, alcohol same. Only 200 Kroner gifts.
Poland	200 cigarettes/50 cigars/250g tobacco/1 litre spirits/1 litre wine
Portugal *	200 cigarettes/50 cigars/250g tobacco/1 litre spirits/2 litres wine/50g perfume/7500 Escudos gifts
Romania	200 cigarettes/300g tobacco/2 litres spirits/4 litres wine or beer/ROL 2000 gifts
Russia	250 cigarettes/250g tobacco/1 litre spirits/2 litres wine/small amount of perfume/30 Roubles gifts
Slovak Republic	250 cigarettes/500g perfume/1litre spirits/2 litres wine/CSK500 gifts
Spain *	200 cigarettes/50 cigars/250g tobacco/1 litre spirits/2 litres wine/50g perfume/5000 Pesetas gifts. Double tobacco allowance if arriving from outside Europe or Mediterranean countries.
Sweden *	200 cigarettes/50 cigars/250g tobacco/1 litre spirits/2 litres wine/small amount perfume/1000 Kroner gifts
Switzerland	200 cigarettes/50 cigars/250g tobacco/1 litre spirits/2 litres wine or beer. 400 cigarettes if resident outside Europe.
Ukraine	N/A
United Kingdom	200 cigarettes/50 cigars/1 litre spirits/2 litres wine/£36 gifts

*Denotes EU member country. Imports of duty-paid goods from other countries are not restricted, save to a reasonable quantity for personal use.

Fig. 3. *(continued)*.

- Keep receipts for items you have purchased recently, especially goods bought duty-paid.

- *Never* be tempted to smuggle.

- Always co-operate fully with any random checks.

DEALING WITH EMERGENCIES

In an emergency
In an **emergency** the procedure should always be:

- Stay calm.

- Decide exactly what help is needed.

- Summon assistance (police, fire, doctor *etc*).

- As soon as possible, inform your emergency contact at home.

- In case of accident, becoming the victim of a crime or a medical emergency, contact your insurance company. They may have an emergency assistance service.

Getting help from the police
Whenever you first arrive in a new country you should acquaint yourself with the local police service and how to make use of it in an emergency. The system may be very different to what you are used to.

In all European countries the police can be summoned in an emergency by telephoning 112.

If you wish to contact the police in a non-emergency situation then you should remember that in some countries there are often several police forces, usually:

- **Paramilitary police**: Deal with major crime, bank robberies, riots and so on. They do not usually help tourists.

- **Municipal police**: Deal with petty crime, muggings, parking offences.

- **Local police**: Deal with crime in the country, and are sometimes part of the army.

● **Customs police**: Patrol borders and deal with smuggling.

Some countries, such as Greece, also have tourist police.

If in doubt about whom to contact ask at a tourist office or any hotel.

You should *not* normally expect ordinary police officers to speak English. In some countries officers speaking English and other languages may be available. They often wear badges showing the flags of the nations whose language they speak.

Attitudes of foreign police forces vary. In some countries they are friendly and helpful. In others they are unfriendly: if you have a reason for requiring their help (such as to report a theft) you may have to insist that they make out a report.

Getting medical assistance

In all European countries an ambulance or doctor can be summoned in an emergency by telephoning 112.

If the situation is not an emergency first try to contact a local doctor. They will be able to either assist or refer you to someone who can. If not, go to a hospital.

To find out where the nearest suitable hospital is tourist offices are usually able to help. If not, then any local hotel will usually know if and where English speaking assistance is available.

Note that in many countries both public and private doctors, dentists and hospitals exist. If you use a private hospital you will be expected to pay the bill, for which you will have to have insurance. So, before using such facilities always ask whether they are private or public, and if public, check that they can treat you under any national health scheme (more details about this are given later).

Getting help from the embassy

The help available to travellers from the **embassy** or **consulate** of your country is actually quite limited.

A consul *can*:

● Issue emergency passports if yours is lost or stolen.

● Contact friends and relatives at home if you need help in an emergency (for example, if you need them to send you money).

● Issue emergency funds up to £50 against a UK cheque and banker's card.

● Provide a list of local doctors, lawyers and interpreters.

● Ensure you are dealt with according to the law if you are arrested. (They can give you details of a local lawyer but cannot pay for it).

A consul can give you an emergency loan (for example, to travel home) but only in a severe emergency. Note that they are not obliged to do this.

A consul *cannot*:

● pay any hotel, legal or medical bills for you
● pay for any travel tickets unless as above
● give legal advice or interfere in local legal systems
● investigate a crime
● help you to find work or get any work/residence permits
● get favourable treatment for you, by the police or in a hospital
● help make travel arrangements or solve other problems.

Note that if you have dual nationality the embassy of your first country cannot help you at all when you are in the country of your second nationality, and vice versa.

If you need the services of the embassy the best procedure is always to telephone first. The local tourist office, police and many hostels know of the number. *Do not* travel in person in the first instance. The embassy will tell you what to do next: there may be a consulate or honorary consulate locally who can help you.

Embassies usually follow local business hours. Out of these hours a recorded message will tell you how to obtain help in an emergency.

FINDING OUT ABOUT ENTERTAINMENT

What's going on?
Entertainment is, of course, part of any trip. To get the best from this always plan ahead.

If you write or 'phone the tourist office of the country concerned before leaving home you should normally be able to get free details of **'what's on?'** and, possibly, a **calendar of events** during your stay.

If you have a special interest *eg* birdwatching or theatre it can be worth writing to the relevant organisations in the country you wish to visit *before* leaving home so that you can then plan ahead.

Finally, tourist guides are always well worth considering. To save the expense and weight of taking numerous books obtain them from libraries and make notes covering only what you really want to see and do.

On arrival at your destination always ask the local tourist office for details of 'what's on?'. Large hotels also often have information, and you do not need to be a guest to obtain this help. Also look for local universities and colleges and see if they have an entertainments office.

Getting free entertainment
Entertainment can be expensive in any country. There are, however, several ways you can enjoy yourself for little or no cost:

● Contact universities and colleges to see what concerts may be on.

● Look for bars and clubs which have free bands (make sure the drinks are not priced up).

● Many countries offer free admission to public buildings, museums, archaelogical sites. Take advantage of them.

● Buy tickets, *eg* for the theatre, at the last minute or look for 'unwanted tickets for sale' in the local papers.

● If you are really keen on a particular activity which is beyond your budget then contact the manager and introduce yourself as a 'foreign student undertaking research'. With a little persuasion they may let you in free!

Getting discounts
● Always take your student ID card if you have one. If you don't have one try offering your bus pass or other form of ID with photograph. It often works!

● Ask for a student discount even if one is not advertised.

● Ask about group discounts which are often generous. If your group isn't large enough then approach other backpackers at your hotel/hostel or around town and see if you can get a group together.

● Get to know your fellow travellers. Buy the unused portion of 'all in' or 'multisaver' tickets from those who do not wish to use them.

Meeting the locals
When you're travelling abroad it's always a good idea to make a special effort to meet the locals. Not only does this give you an extra taste of the **local culture** but you can also find out much useful information from local people, such as worthwhile places to go and things to see, and also where to buy things much cheaper than most other tourists have to pay. Also, when you meet the locals, you will find that many stereotypes regarding different nationalities are proved wrong.

The best way of meeting the locals is to try and get off the beaten track: back street cafes, bars and so on are all good places to meet people, as are local universities and colleges. In any country you will, of course, find conmen (and women) but these usually only comprise a tiny percentage of the population as a whole. You will usually meet the most genuine people by approaching them on their territory. *Be more cautious*, however, about offers of help or friendship made in tourist places and also airports, railway stations, ports and the like.

UNDERSTANDING INSURANCE

What you need to be covered for
Don't forget to get insured before you travel. In fact, it's a good idea to take out your insurance as soon as you have decided to go. This way it will be all paid for well in advance – and you will also be covered if for some reason you have to cancel your trip.

Remember that you are more likely to suffer an accident or theft when you are abroad then you are at home! (But don't let that put you off going!)

Here is what you should be covered for:

- **Medical treatment**: Whilst it is true that nationals of many countries worldwide can get free emergency medical treatment in many European countries under a reciprocal agreement it is not really a good idea to rely on this. Facilities are often overcrowded and difficult to find and, in some countries, may be of poor quality. If you have medical insurance you will be able to use any hospital, even a private one.

- **Personal accident**: This is quite different from medical insurance. If for example, you are involved in an accident such as a traffic accident or a fall, this will cover your expenses and provide compensation.

- **Baggage insurance**: This will cover theft, loss or accidental damage to your possessions. Go for a policy which will provide an immediate cash sum if an incident occurs. This way you will be able to replace your possessions immediately.

- **Legal expenses**: Will pay for legal assistance if you are arrested or some claim is made against you.

Getting affordable insurance
There is a very wide range of travel insurance schemes available today. They vary widely in price and coverage so best check a selection and go for one that offers the best coverage at the lowest price.

If you are staying away for more than a month it may be a good idea to consider an annual travel insurance policy which will work out cheaper than a month-by-month policy. These policies are sold by some banks and building societies. American Express also offer a competitively priced annual insurance policy (Tel: (01273) 693555).

Useful tips
- If you intend to work remember that most travel insurance policies are intended for holiday-makers and so will not cover you whilst at work. When working you should be covered by your employer's insurance although not all have this.

- If you intend to undertake any dangerous sports remember that a standard travel insurance policy may not cover you. If it does you may have to pay an additional premium. Most travel insurance companies include skiing, parascending and scuba diving as dangerous sports.

LANGUAGES

Coping with the language barrier
When travelling around Europe you will find that although some people do speak English, *most people do not*. This is particularly the case if you wish to backpack away from capital cities and resorts.

Also remember that even where local people do speak English they probably prefer to speak their own language wherever possible. You will get a much better reception if you can communicate with them in their own language.

It is well worth brushing up on your language skills before leaving home. Here are some ways of learning:

- *Evening classes*: Are available in most areas and are fairly cheap. Ask your local further education institute.

- *Audio cassette courses:* These can give you a good basic knowledge but they can be quite expensive. Look for second-hand courses for sale in local newspapers.

- *Private tuition*: A few hours with a native speaker of the language you wish to learn could be worthwhile. This is a good option for the most obscure languages in which evening classes are rarely offered. Look in the local papers or place a 'tuition wanted' advertisement.

- *Summer schools*: Some European universities run language courses during the vacations. These courses are inexpensive and you often have the opportunity to live with a local family too. For example, some French universities run summer schools. For details ask the embassy of the country you plan to visit.

Figure 4 is a list of the languages spoken around Europe and Figure 5 is a list of useful phrases to learn before you set off on your trip.

FINDING OUT ABOUT MEDICAL TREATMENT AND HOSPITALS

Getting free treatment

Many of the countries in Europe have reciprocal agreements with other European countries and elsewhere in the world which allow visitors to obtain **free emergency medical treatment** in that country.

The countries which currently have reciprocal agreements are:

- All the European Union (EU) countries: Austria, Belgium, Denmark, Finland, France, Germany, Greece, Ireland, Italy, Luxembourg, Netherlands, Portugal, Spain, Sweden and the UK.

Plus:

- Belarus, Bulgaria, Czech Republic, Estonia, Hungary, Latvia, Lithuania, Norway, Poland, Romania, Russia, Slovak Republic, and also the Channel Islands and Isle of Man.

If you are travelling *from* one of these countries to *any* of the other countries in the list you will be able to get some free emergency medical treatment in that country.

If you take advantage of this arrangement there are three points that you should bear in mind. Firstly, free treatment may be difficult to obtain in some countries as it may be rationed and you may have to wait. Secondly, it may be of a poor standard and finally, *not everything* may be free. You may have to pay, for example, for drugs and hospital accommodation charges. For this reason we do recommend that you take out private medical insurance to provide treatment in the best available hospital locally, whether public or private.

If you intend to claim free treatment here is what to do:

● If travelling to an EU country you should take with you **form E111**. This is available from post offices. You will need to produce your E111 in order to claim free treatment.

● If travelling to a non-EU country produce your passport to claim free treatment.

Twelve useful health tips

Here are twelve important matters you should consider when travelling around Europe.

1. **HIV and AIDS**: The HIV virus is present, and cases of infection are increasing, in every European country. The main ways of catching the virus are sexual contact with an infected person, sharing infected needles when misusing illegal drugs and from medical or dental equipment which has been inadequately sterilised. Take the same precautions you would at home.

2. **Rabies**: Rabies is present throughout all of Europe except the UK and Ireland, although the risk is minimal in most places. Just in case, the best precaution is to avoid coming into contact with any animal, especially wild and stray animals. If you are bitten by any animal clean the wound immediately with soap and water, seek medical advice and inform the police.

3. **Sunburn**: Remember that the sun becomes stronger the further south you travel. If you wish to sunbathe always use a sunscreen cream and, preferably, stay out of the sun altogether during the hottest part of the day (noon-3pm).

Country	Main language spoken	English spoken?
Albania	Albanian. Greek also spoken	No
Austria	Austrian, German	Sometimes
Baltic States		
Estonia	Estonian Russian	
Latvia	Latvian also	
Lithuania	Lithuanian spoken	No
Belarus	Belarussian Russian also spoken	No
Belgium	French and Flemish	Yes in Brussels
Bulgaria	Bulgarian	No
Czech Republic	Czech	No
Denmark	Danish	Sometimes
Finland	Finnish and Swedish in some parts	Sometimes
France	French	In cities
Germany	German	Sometimes
Greece	Greek	In resorts
Hungary	Hungarian	No
Ireland	Gaelic and English	Yes
Italy	Italian	No
Luxembourg	Mostly German	Sometimes
Netherlands	Dutch	Sometimes
Norway	Norwegian	Sometimes
Poland	Polish	No
Portugal	Portuguese	In resorts
Romania	Romanian	No
Russia	Russian	No
Slovak Republic	Slovak	No
Spain	Spanish	In resorts
Sweden	Swedish	Sometimes
Switzerland	French, German, Italian	Sometimes
Ukraine	Ukranian	No
United Kingdom	English	Yes

Fig. 4. Languages spoken around Europe.

GB – Do you speak English?

F – Parlez vous anglais?

D – Sprechen Sie Englisch?

I – Parla Inglese?

E – Habla Ingles?

P – Fala Ingles?

GB - Good morning

F – Bonjour

D – Guten Morgen

I – Buongiorno

E – Buenos Días

P – Bom dia

GB – Goodbye

F – Au revoir

D – Auf Wiedersehen

I – Arrivederci!

E – ¡Adios!

P – Adeus

GB – Hello

F – Bonjour

D – Guten Tag

I – Ciao

E – ¡Hola!

P – Olá

GB – How are you?

F – Comment-allez vous?

D – Wie geht es Ihnen?

I – Come sta?

E – Como esta?

P – Como está?

GB – I am very pleased to meet you

F – Enchanté

D – Angenehm

I – Piacere. Leito di conoscerla.

E – Mucho gusto

P – Muito prazer

GB – I don't speak ...

F – Je ne parle pas ...

D – Ich spreche kein ...

I – Non parlo ...

E – No hablo ...

P – Não falo ...

GB – My name is ...

F – Je m'appelle ...

D – Ich heiße ...

I – Mi chiamo ...

E – Me llamo ...

P – Chamo-me ...

Fig. 5. A list of useful phrases.

GB – No	GB – Please
F – Non	F – S'il vous plait
D – Nein	D – Bitte
I – No	I – Per favore
E – No	E – Por favor
P – Não	P – Se faz favor
GB – Thank you	GB – Where is the ...?
F – Merci	F – Où es ...
D – Danke	D – Wo ist ...
I – Grazie	I – Dov'è ...
E – Gracias	E – Dondé está
P – Obrigado/a	P – Onde é a ...
GB – Yes	GB – You're welcome
F – Oui	F – Je vous en prie
D – Ja	D – Bitte sehr
I – Si	I – Prego
E – Si	E – De nada
P – Sim	P – De nada

Key:

GB – English	I – Italian
F – French	E - Spanish
D – German	P - Portuguese

Fig. 5. *(continued)*.

4. **Food safety**: The chance of contracting food poisoning varies
    from country to country. It tends to be greater in countries with
    lower standards of public hygiene and in warmer climates which,
    coincidentally, tend to be the souther European countries. The
    best way of minimising the risk is always to eat in the cleanest
    establishments you can afford (if the dining area looks dirty the
    kitchens are probably dirtier). Avoid street vendors. Also try to
    eat only food which has been freshly cooked.

5. **Water safety**: Although mains water is supposedly safe to drink in
    all European countries it can easily become contaminated once it
    has left the mains supply. It is best not to drink this water unless
    a reliable person assures you it is safe to do so. Drink bottled
    water and well-known canned drinks where possible. Tap water
    of unknown purity can also be sterilised to kill most bacteria by
    heating it to a temperature of 100°c for at least two minutes.

6. **Traveller's diarrhoea**: If you are worried about the prospect of
    diarrhoea then pack an anti-diarrhoea preparation such as
    loperamide (sold as Arret or Imodium) in your backpack. This
    should only be given to adults. If contracting diarrhoea it is also
    important to drink plenty of clean water as, otherwise,
    dehydration can become a serious problem, especially in warm
    climates. If you suffer bloody diarrhoea and severe abdominal
    pain you should seek medical help.

7. **Insect hazards:** Serious insect-borne diseases do not exist
    anywhere in Europe, east or west. Many places in southern
    Europe are plagued by mosquitoes and although these,
    fortunately, do not carry malaria their bites can still result in
    uncomfortable, itchy wounds. If visiting such places take an
    insect repellent. Also keep as much skin as possible covered
    during the night, which is when mosquitoes bite.
        Ticks which transmit **tick-borne encephalitis** (TBE) are present
    in some forested areas, mainly in Scandinavia, in summer. If
    visiting such areas use an insect repellent and keep skin covered
    when walking or hiking.

8. **Snakes**: You shouldn't encounter any dangerous reptiles in any
    part of Europe. However, it is always a good idea to avoid all wild
    animal life when travelling in any country.

9. **Sea dangers**: The main sea hazards for swimmers and watersports enthusiasts in Europe are pollution and sea life, such as jellyfish and stonefish. The best way to avoid these risks is to only swim on lifeguard patrolled beaches, which are usually also free from pollution and most animal hazards, especially in locations which the locals use. Avoid swimming in all rivers and lakes.

    Finally, remember that many severe injuries are caused every year to those who dive into the sea, rivers, lakes and swimming pools which are too shallow.

10. **Sporting dangers**: You may wish to pursue your favourite sports whilst travelling. Remember, however, that safety standards leave much to be desired in some parts of Europe, especially around the Mediterranean. If you wish to go parascending, skiing, waterskiing, scuba diving *etc*, always use a reputable club or school. Make sure your insurance covers you for these – most policies do not unless you pay an extra premium.

11. **Dehydration**: If travelling from a cool climate to a warm one remember that dehydration can occur very quickly and, in extreme cases, can develop into a severe medical condition. Always ensure your intake of fluids is adequate. In a hot climate you should normally aim to consume at least 10 litres of clean water (as opposed to alcohol or fruit drinks) per 24 hours.

12. **Travel sickness**: The best way to avoid travel sickness is to sleep as much as possible during the journey. Avoid reading. Suitable medicines you could try include **Dramamine**, **Stugeron** and **Kwells**. If you are especially prone to travel sickness you could ask your doctor about **Scopoderm skin patches**.

Using hospitals
Here is what you need to do to obtain medical treatment when abroad:

● In a serious emergency, **call an ambulance**.

If the incident is not a serious emergency, proceed as follows:

● If you have private medical insurance telephone your insurance company. Most have a 24 hour assistance number and will accept reverse-charge calls.

- If you do not have private medical insurance contact your local hospitals. Ask if they are public hospitals and accept patients under the state health scheme. If they do, you may be able to use them free of charge under a reciprocal agreement as already discussed. If they do not you will have to pay the bill in full. This will usually be extremely costly, even for minor treatment, so be warned.

Claiming free treatment with an E111

Earlier in this section we discussed how you may be able to use the **E111 form** system to obtain some free medical treatment in Europe. Here is exactly how to use this system in each EU country:

- **Belgium**: If not an emergency go to the sickness insurance office who will issue a certificate for free treatment and direct you to a hospital.

- **Denmark**: Show your passport or E111 to the hospital authorities.

- **France**: Go directly to hospital. If you are treated as an in-patient you will have to pay the cost and then reclaim it from the local sickness insurance office (**caisse primaire d'assurance maladie**).

- **Germany**: If not an emergency obtain clearance from the local sickness insurance office (**AOK**) first.

- **Greece**: Ask the local **IKA** office for a hospital voucher. For an emergency go directly to hospital.

- **Ireland**: Go to any health service hospital and tell them you are resident in another EU country.

- **Italy**: Show your E111 to the hospital authorities and ask them to arrange free treatment.

- **Luxembourg**: Show your E111 to the hospital authorities and ask them to arrange free treatment.

- **Netherlands**: You, or your doctor, must obtain authorisation from **ANOZ (Algemeen Nederlands Onderling Ziekenfonds)** before hospital treatment.

- **Portugal**: Show your E111 or passport to the hospital.

- **Spain**: Show your E111 to the hospital. It is useful if you have a photocopy to give them.

- **United Kingdom**: Show your E111 to the hospital.

Vaccinations
No vaccinations are either compulsory or recommended for any destination within Europe, including eastern Europe.

If you are travelling in remote areas or intend to work then it is a good idea to ensure that you have a tetanus vaccinations.

THINKING ABOUT MONEY

Managing your money
There are several different ways to take your spending money when backpacking in Europe:

- **Traveller's cheques**: These are available at all banks, post offices and many travel agencies and can simply be exchanged for cash in the local currency in every European country. Sterling cheques are accepted in all European countries. Ask for many small denominations so that you do not have too much money left over when leaving one country and then have to pay again to convert it into the currency of the next country.

- **Eurocheques**: with a Eurocheque card you can simply make out cheques using your regular cheque book to pay for goods and services in shops, hotels and so on in every European country. These are safe, convenient and easy. However, you do have to pay a fee on each cheque used, so they are better used only for larger purposes.

- **Cash dispenser cards**: Cash cards issued by most banks are now acceptable at many cash dispenser machines in European countries. Ask your bank which networks their card is valid in. Although a handling charge is made for these cash withdrawals you will find it is quite economic compared to other methods. The only difficulty, however, may be in finding a cash machine if travelling in rural areas.

- **Credit cards**: If you do not have a credit card it is worth considering applying for one. Visa and Mastercard are accepted in all European countries. They can be used in shops, to pay for travel and accommodation, and can also be used in banks and cash dispensers to withdraw cash. Again, a handling fee is charged on cash withdrawals but it compares favourably with other methods.

   If you do not wish to run up a large credit bill then it is still worth having a credit card to provide an emergency fund. Alternatively, pay your spending money into the card account before you travel.

- **Cash**: It is never a good idea to take your spending money in cash. Remember, as a backpacker you are more likely to suffer a loss or theft in any case so only carry as much cash as you need at any one time.

Changing money

Using a bank may be a little different to what you are used to at home. Firstly, always check up on the business and bank hours in the country you wish to visit. These are listed elsewhere in this chapter.

Banks usually charge transaction fees on currency exchange and do not always offer the best interest rates, but they are usually reliable and honest when calculating the transaction. In some countries the bank will have a doorman. Ask them exactly where to go as there is often a separate department for currency exchange. Always take your passport when changing currency. It may not always be required, but it sometimes is.

Bureaux de change offices may offer a better exchange rate but may charge a transaction fee also. Before using them calculate whether the end deal will be better or worse than a bank. Also, work out for yourself what currency you should receive and check your change carefully as dishonesty is a risk in some places. Do not use unlicensed moneychangers. They may offer a better rate but are very often dishonest.

PACKING

What to pack

Here is a checklist of some basic essentials you won't want to forget. Use it when you're packing.

Documents
- passport ☐

Country	Currency	Divided into:	Currency controls?
Albania	Leks	-	Y
Austria	Schilling	100 Groschen	Y
Baltic States			
Estonia	Kroon	100 Cents	Y
Latvia	Lat	100 Santimi	Y
Lithuania	Litas	100 Centu	Y
Belarus	Rubel	10 Rub	Y
Belgium	Belgian Franc	100 Centimes	N
Bulgaria	Lev	100 Stotinki	Y
Czech Republic	Koruna	100 Haleru	Y
Denmark	Krone	100 Ore	Y
Finland	Markka	100 Pennia	N
France	Franc	100 Centimes	Y
Germany	Mark	100 Pfennigs	N
Greece	Drachma	-	Y
Hungary	Forint	100 Filler	Y
Ireland	Punt	100 Pence	Y
Italy	Lira	-	N
Luxembourg	Lux. Franc	100 Centimes	N
Netherlands	Guilder	100 Cents	N
Norway	Krone	100 Ore	Y
Poland	Zloty	100 Groszny	N
Portugal	Escudo	100 Centavos	Y
Romania	Leu	100 Bani	Y
Russia	Rouble	-	Y
Slovak Republic	Koruna	100 Haleru	Y
Spain	Peseta	-	N
Sweden	Krona	100 Ore	N
Switzerland	Swiss Franc	-	N
Ukraine	Karbovanets	-	Y
United Kingdom	Pound	100 Pence	N

(Y=Yes, imports and exports of local currency are limited. Ask a bank for details. N=No limits to imports and exports.)

Fig. 6. Guide to currencies around Europe.

- insurance certificate ☐
- cash and traveller's cheques ☐
- ID cards ☐
- travel tickets ☐

Medicines/first aid
- travel sickness remedies ☐
- anti-diarrhoea remedies ☐
- prescription medicines (if any) ☐
- painkillers ☐
- insect repellant ☐
- antiseptic cream ☐
- bandages and plasters ☐
- sun block ☐

Luggage
- backpack ☐
- day pack ☐
- sleeping bag ☐
- sleeping mat ☐
- camping equipment (if camping) ☐

Clothing
- walking boots ☐
- trainers ☐
- jeans/trousers ☐
- t-shirts ☐
- jacket/pullover ☐
- shorts ☐
- swimming costume ☐
- waterproof clothing ☐
- underwear ☐
- sun hat ☐

Other items
- toiletries ☐
- camera ☐
- sports equipment ☐
- phrase books/maps/guides ☐
- reading material ☐

Useful tips
Here are some tips that will save you time, space and money when backpacking:

- Think about where you are travelling and pack accordingly. In souther Europe you are unlikely to need any warm clothing in mid-summer since it is warm even if it rains.

- Buy any clothes you need well in advance. It's best if you feel comfortable in what you wear, especially shoes and boots *etc.*

- Look for second-hand bargains in backpacks, camping equipment so on. You might not use it again.

- Don't take any expensive items of clothing or designer brands. You may attract petty thieves.

- If space is tight always pack the heavier and more expensive items such as shoes, boots and jeans first. These will cost you a lot to buy *en route* if you leave them out. Items like T-shirts, on the other hand, can be bought cheaply in any country.

- If travelling to a cool climate take many layers of thin clothing rather than just one item of thick clothing. These are easier to carry, easier to launder and easier to adjust to the prevailing temperature.

- Choose either thin cotton clothing or items with a high man-made fibre content. These are lighter, easier to wash and quicker to dry. Avoid thick woollen items.

- If travelling by air, weigh your luggage carefully to avoid excess charges. Most airlines permit only 25Kg for economy class passengers.

- Where possible, choose cheap items of clothing and equipment that you can throw away (or even sell) when you have finished with them.

GETTING PASSPORTS, PERMITS AND VISAS

Obtaining a passport

A passport is recommended for all journeys within Europe. Although citizens of some EU countries do not need them for journeys to other EU countries you will certainly need them for journeys outside the EU. Since you may wish to change your itinerary it is best to apply for a full passport.

British citizens should note that a full passport is required to travel to mainland Europe. The British visitor's passport is no longer valid.

In the UK, passport application forms can be obtained from your nearest main post office. The application can then be returned direct to the passport office. If you wish applications can be lodged at post offices and certain nominated travel agents who will check the application before sending it to the passport office.

Apply in plenty of time – at least twelve weeks before you wish to go abroad – longer if you wish to visit a country that requires a visa.

Obtaining visas

EU citizens travelling to another EU country do not need any sort of **visa**. The EU countries are Austria, Belgium, Denmark, Finland, France, Germany, Greece, Ireland, Italy, Luxembourg, Netherlands, Portugal, Spain, Sweden and the UK.

EU citizens travelling outside the EU *may* need a visa, even if travelling as a tourist. (If you intend to work, a visa will *definitely* be needed.) More information on whether visas are required for these countries is given in Chapter 6.

Non-EU citizens may require a visa to visit any of the countries (EU and non-EU) covered in this book. Since regulations are complex and liable to change you should check with the embassies of the countries you wish to visit.

If a visa is needed you can often obtain them at the border but it is usually easier to get them in your own country before leaving home. Apply to the relevant embassy. Most embassies issue visas by post but require at least four weeks' notice. If there is insufficient time you can often apply by going to the embassy (check opening times before travelling as they often open their visa sections only part-time) or use a visa service – although this can be expensive.

It is a good idea to obtain visas for any countries which require them if you simply *think* you might visit them. It will save time later. Some visa agencies in London are:

Rapid Visa Service, 131–135 Earls Court Road, London SW5 9RH. Tel: (0171) 373 3026.

Thames Consular Services, 363 Chiswick High Road, London W4 4HS. Tel: (0181) 995 2492.

Thomas Cook Passport and Visa Service, 45 Berkeley Street, London W1A 1EB. Tel: (0171) 408 4141.

Obtaining work and residence permits

Information about work permits – if you intend to work – is given in Chapter 5.

If you are taking a longer trip you should note that, although EU citizens do not require permits to visit or work in other EU countries, they do require residence permits if staying for over three months. These can be obtained at the local town hall, police station or alien's office. You will need to produce evidence that you have sufficient financial means to support yourself (*ie* money in a bank account) although this amount varies from country to country.

CONSIDERING SAFETY AND SECURITY

Europe is generally a safe part of the world in which to travel. However, the situation varies from country to country. More advice is given on this later.

It is always wise to take precautions when travelling if only because travellers are more liable to accidents and crime, just because they are travellers.

If you need to find out the latest security position before travelling to a particular country ask your travel agent.

Special precautions need to be taken by female travellers. It is inadvisable to travel alone in all but a few countries, and even then take care. **Do not hitchhike**, and think twice about accepting offers of food, drink, transport, accommodation or jobs from strangers.

Do's and don'ts

Do have a planned itinerary and 'report in' from time to time with someone back at home.

Do take proper insurance at all times.

Do keep emergency contact addresses in a safe place and with you at all times.

Do remember that situations vary from country to country *and* between rural and urban areas. For example, many rural areas of France have hardly any crime whereas cities can be dangerous.

Don't deviate from your itinerary without telling someone.

Don't get split up from your friends without arranging a meeting time and place.

Don't carry any more money than you have to at any one time.

Don't carry anything of any real value or that is irreplaceable.

Twenty tips to help you keep safe

Here are twenty more tips you will find useful to keep you safe and secure during your trip:

1. Be very wary about hitchhiking. Only hitchhike in pairs if possible. Even in countries that are regarded as safe avoid hitchhiking at night.

2. Pay a little more for a decent hotel with good security rather than a cheap hotel.

3. Be careful about sleeping on trains.

4. Take a lock and chain to secure your luggage when travelling.

5. Always keep your money and travel documents on your person, not in your luggage. A money belt may seem silly but it is the best idea.

6. Learn to 'read' your surroundings. If a particular town or street looks run down then it probably has a crime problem.

7. When first arriving in a new place take a taxi or bus rather than walking.

8.   Avoid parks and beaches at night.

9.   Do not wear jewellery, or show expensive watches or cameras.

10. Always carry bags around your shoulder if possible, never in your hand.

11. Avoid offers of food or drink from people in the street (and especially on trains). Drugged food is used by some criminals.

12. Avoid seedy or dubious-looking bars.

13. Avoid illegal activities such as drugs, unofficial money changing, illegal gambling and so on. Quite apart from the fact they are illegal these activities are even more risky when in unfamiliar surroundings than they are at home.

14. Never carry packages for people you do not know, especially through ports and airports.

15. Carry your backpack as little as possible as this identifies you as a tourist. Stow it at stations if you are exploring a new city.

16. Always take advice or directions from a trustworthy person, such as a tourist office official, uniformed airline/bus company official.

17. A personal attack alarm is a good idea.

18. If attacked it is not usually a good idea to resist or to fight back. However, shouting or screaming loudly such as 'Help!' or 'Police!' in the appropriate local language is enough to deter some petty criminals.

19. Be especially careful when visiting the most popular tourist sites. These are often the most popular with petty criminals too.

20. Women should be particularly quick to repel unwanted advances, or they may rapidly develop into a serious problem. Firstly, ignore the offender. If this fails a firm rebuff using the worst language you can think of should work. If not, a loud scream or slap across the face should be effective. Do not engage in any conversation.

Country	Safety tips
Albania	Once very safe, crime has risen lately.
Austria	Very safe.
Baltic States	Reasonably safe.
Belarus	Mostly safe, but take care.
Belgium	Safe.
Bulgaria	Petty crime is increasing.
Czech Republic	Fairly safe.
Denmark	Very safe.
Finland	Very safe.
France	Safe, petty crime a problem in cities.
Germany	Safe.
Greece	Safe.
Hungary	Fairly safe.
Ireland	Safe.
Italy	Petty crime a problem in cities.
Luxembourg	Safe.
Netherlands	Safe.
Norway	Very safe.
Poland	Crime is increasing.
Portugal	Safe, some petty crime.
Romania	Fairly safe.
Russia	Crime is increasing.
Slovak Republic	Fairly safe.
Spain	Petty crime a problem in some places.
Sweden	Very safe.
Switzerland	Very safe.
Ukraine	Crime is increasing.
United Kingdom	Safe.

Fig. 7. Safety and security around Europe.

SHOPPING

Buying it cheaper

No matter how carefully you try to pack there will always be those things you cannot take with you and, of course, those things you forget. If you are on a limited budget you will want to obtain them as cheaply as possible so here are some tips on how to go about it.

Think twice about buying anything **duty free**, as it may be duty free but is rarely much cheaper at the end of the day. Similarly, avoid shops in tourist spots and major shopping streets.

It can pay to look for well-known discount chains (*eg Monoprix* in France). These usually offer cheap prices combined with reasonable quality. Alternatively, shop in small stores where you can bargain with the owner. In such places always offer to pay cash in return for a discount.

Buying from street traders and markets can be extremely cheap but check the quality of the goods *before* paying and *check your change carefully*. If buying large or costly items, such as a backpack, look for second-hand items in local newspapers or on notice boards.

Finally, use discount cards wherever possible. These are listed elsewhere.

Eating cheaply

Avoid buying too many snacks as they are usually more expensive than full meals.

As a general rule, avoid well-known fast food outlets. However, some of them do have special off-peak and promotional offers which are good value. Look for cafeterias in universities and colleges. They are sometimes open to students from all countries. Also, try back street cafés used by locals.

Look for 'all you can eat' deals which are popular in some countries. Or take the fixed price menu which is nearly always a bargain!

If you are really stuck, try soup kitchens and charity diners.

Shopping for gifts and souvenirs

First of all, **always shop around** since prices of souvenir items can vary considerably. Avoid swish gift and souvenir shops which are always overpriced.

A good idea is to select something that you can use yourself on your trip and then give as a gift. Also, look for unusual 'free' souvenirs, such as pressed wild flowers or sea shells (but note some countries forbid the taking of rocks or pebbles from ancient sites). Photographs are some of the cheapest gifts and souvenirs available and are always appreciated by people at home.

Rather than lug around difficult-to-carry gifts and souvenirs send them back home by parcel post. Surface mail needn't cost much and they may well reach home before you.

If your budget is really tight then tickets, leaflets, receipted bills and postcards make a unique momento of your trip.

Figure 8 details the different business and shopping hours across Europe.

Country	Business hours
Albania	Varies
Austria	0800–1800 Mon–Fri with 2 hour lunch break. 0800–1200 Sat.
Baltic States	Varies
Belarus	1100–2000 daily.
Belgium	0900–1800 every day.
Bulgaria	0800–1800 Mon–Sat.
Czech Republic	0900–1800 Mon–Fri, lunch 1200–1400. 0900–1200 Sat.
Denmark	0900–1730 Mon–Thu. 0900–1900 Fri. 0900–1200 Sat.
Finland	0800–2000 Mon–Fri. 0800–1800 Sat.
France	0900–1930 Mon–Sat. (All day Monday closing still common.)
Germany	0900–1800 Mon–Fri. 0800–1300 Sat.
Greece	0800–1400 and 1700–2000 Mon–Sat.

Fig. 8. Business and shopping hours around Europe.

Country	Business hours
Hungary	1000–1800 Mon–Fri. 0900–1200 Sat.
Ireland	0900–1730 Mon–Sat.
Italy	0900–1300 and 1600–2000 Mon–Sat.
Luxembourg	0800–1200 and 1400–1800 Mon–Sat. (Monday morning closing is common.)
Netherlands	0800–1200 and 1400–1800 Mon–Sat.
Norway	0900–1700 Mon–Sat.
Poland	1100–1900 daily. (Food shops may open as early as 0700.)
Portugal	0900–1300 and 1500–1900 Mon–Fri. 0900–1300 Sat.
Romania	Varies
Russia	1100–2000 daily.
Slovak Republic	0900–1200 and 1600–1800 Mon–Fri. 0900–1200 Sat.
Spain	0900–1330 and 1500–2000 daily.
Sweden	0930–1730 Mon–Fri. 0930–1400 Sat.
Switzerland	0800–1800 Mon–Fri. 0800–1600 Sat. (Monday closing is usual.)
Ukraine	Varies
United Kingdom	0900–1730 Mon–Sat.

(Business hours do not usually include Saturday.)

Fig. 8. *(continued)*.

5
Working Your Way Round Europe

Working as you go can be a very good idea. Not only will this help fund your travels, but it will really help you to experience the culture of the country concerned to a much greater extent than you can as a tourist.

Most European countries have many opportunities for casual work. However, remember that there is also a great deal of competition for this work from other travellers, especially in summer, so it may be very hard to find a vacancy. Also, if you do not speak the language of the country concerned it will be much harder to find work.

In this chapter we will look at some of the opportunities, explain how to find them, and also explain what permits you may need.

GETTING CASUAL WORK

Possible casual jobs
Most travellers look for casual work, which requires few skills or commitment. Here are some of the jobs you could consider:

Farm work
Farmers often need a few extra pairs of hands, especially at busy times such as harvest or planting. Pay is usually low but you might get benefits such as free food and accommodation.

Child care
You might be able to work as an au pair or nanny. You stand a better chance of getting this work if you are prepared to stay for a few weeks.

Voluntary work projects
Examples of this kind of work include conservation, working with children, working with the elderly and so on. You probably won't be paid for this type of work but you will usually get free food and accommodation.

Building sites
Building sites in most countries often have demand for casual labourers. Make sure they operate to reasonable standards of safety.

Bars
Bars are always in need of part-time workers. This is an ideal type of work in tourist resorts. Do note, however, that the popular resorts have more than enough workers in the high season.

Hotels
Hotels are enthusiastic hirers of casual workers. You may be employed as a chambermaid, gardener, porter and so on. If you can speak the local language you may be able to get a job in reception.

Restaurants
Restaurants often need a lot of staff. You may get work as a kitchen porter or washer-up. Again, if you speak the local language you may get a job as a waiter or waitress or as a meeter-and-greeter.

Shop work
Shops often offer part-time and temporary work in the season. It may be difficult to get this work unless you speak the local language except, of course, if you work in tourist shops where your foreign language knowledge may be invaluable.

Jobs on boats
There are often jobs to be had in harbours and marinas, painting, de-fouling the hull, cleaning and so on. The best way of getting this work is to turn up and ask around.

Touting
If you are a determined type of person you may be able to earn money by persuading tourists to eat in certain restaurants, drink in certain bars or even view timeshare properties. Ask the owners if they need a **tout**.

Selling
In many resorts casual workers are employed to sell drinks, ice creams, sun beds and parasols on the beach. Note that you usually need a licence to do this.

Holiday centres

Holiday centres or camps often have vacancies for chambermaids, waiters and waitresses, porters and so on. If you can sing or dance, or teach a sport, you may even be able to get a job as an entertainer or coach.

Fast-food outlets

Fast-food outlets such as McDonalds exist in almost every European country and often need part-time and temporary staff.

Getting a casual job

Once you have decided you would like to do some casual work there are various methods you can use:

Newspapers

Newspapers are an obvious source of jobs. These are listed later. Apart from the local newspapers of the country concerned some places have English language newspapers which are ideal for English speaking job-hunters. These are also listed later.

Specialised newsletters

In the UK the *Overseas Jobs Express* lists many job opportunities, although many of them are longer term and for those with experience and qualifications to offer. *Overseas Jobs Express* is available on subscription or at many libraries. (It is not available at newsagents.)

National employment services

If you are an EU citizen you can use the state employment service in any other EU country to find a job. However, the extent to which they will help you will depend on whether or not you can speak any or much of the local language.

Private employment agencies

There are private employment agencies in most countries. (In some countries, however, they are not permitted by law.) They may be able to find you a job. You can contact them before you go abroad, although they will probably be in a better position to help you once you are abroad. See the local *Yellow Pages*.

Asking round

There is a lot to be said for the direct approach of job-hunting when looking for casual work. This is because many employers do not have a vacancy as such but are often tempted once help is offered at busy times. So, simply decide what type of work you wish to do and ask away!

Doing research before you go

You can try from home if you wish, although it is better to ask once on the spot. Do your research before you leave home. For example, if you are interested in working in hotels the tourist office may be willing to send you a list of hotels in the locations you intend to travel to.

Useful sources of jobs

Austria
National Employment Services:
- Bebenbergerstrasse 33, 8021 Graz.
- Schopfstrasse 5, Innsbruck.
- Schiesstantestrasse 4, 5021 Salzburg.
- Hohenstauffengasse 2, 1013 Vienna.
- Weihburggasse 30, Vienna.

Belgium
National Employment Service:
- Flanders: VDAB.
- Wallonia: ONEM.
(Offices in most towns.)

Private employment agencies:
- ECCO, 17a Rue Vilian XIV, 1050 Brussels. Tel: 02 647 87 80.
- Avenue Louise Interim, 207 Avenue Louise, 1050 Brussels. Tel: 02 640 91 91.
-Select Interim, 1–5 Avenue de la Joyeuse Entrée, 1040 Brussels. Tel: 02 231 03 33.
-Creyf's, 473 Avenue Louise, 1050 Brussels. Tel: 02 646 34 34.

Bulgaria
-Student Labour Office, PO Box 504, Plovdiv 4000. Tel: 032 226756.

Denmark
National Employment Service:
-Arbejdsformidlingen, Adelgade 13, Copenhagen 1304.

Finland
National Employment Agency:
– Ministry of Labour, Fabianinkatu 32, 00100 Helsinki 10.

France
National Employment Service:
–ANPE, 92136 Issy les Moulineaux, and offices in all towns.

Private employment agencies:
– ECCO, 33 Rue Raffet, 75016 Paris. Tel: 1 45 25 51 51.
– Kelly, 50 Avenue des Champs Elysées, 75008 Paris. Tel: 1 42 56 44 88.
– Manpower, 9 Rue Jacques Bingen, 75017 Paris. Tel: 1 47 66 03 03.

Germany
National Employment Service:
– Arbeitsamt. (Offices in all towns.)
–ZAV, Feuerbachstrasse 42, 6000 Frankfurt Am Main. (If applying from outside Germany.)

Greece
National Employment Service:
– OAED, Thakris 8, 16610 Glyfada, Athens. Tel: 01 993 2589.

Private employment agencies:
– Camenos International Staff Consultancy, 12 Botsai Street, Athens 147.
– Galentinas European Consultancy, PO Box 51181, 14510 Kiffissia, Athens. Tel: 01 1303 1005.
– Intertom Agency, 24–26 Halkokondili Street, Athens 10432. Tel: 01 532 9470.
– Pioneer, 11 Nikis Street, Athens 10557. Tel: 01 322 4321.

Hungary
National Employment Services:
– Katona J. Utca 25, Budapest. Tel: 1 122 294.
– Bokàny D. Utca 2a, Budapest. Tel: 1 124 630.
– Széchenyi Ter 9, Pécs. Tel: 72 13 721.
– Bajcsy Zs. Utca 4, Szeged. Tel: 62 22 890.
– Csaba Utca 26, Györ. Tel: 96 11 180.

Ireland
National Employment Service:
– FÁS, 65a Adelaide Road, Dublin 2. Tel: 01 765861. (Also has local offices in most towns.)

Italy
National Employment Service:
– Ufficio di Collocamento, Mandopera, Via Pastrengo 16, Rome.

Luxembourg
National Employment Service:
– 38a Rue Philippe II, 2340 Luxembourg. Tel: 478 5300.

Netherlands
National Employment Service:
– Singel 202, 1016 AA Amsterdam. Tel: 020 520 0911.
– Begynenhof 8, 5611 EL Eindhoven. Tel: 040 325325.
– Engelse Kamp 4, 9722 AX Groningen. Tel: 050 225911.
– Troelstrakade 65, 2531 AA The Hague.
– Schiedamse Vest 160, 3011 BH Rotterdam.

Private employment agencies:
– Manpower, Van Baerlestraat 16, Amsterdam.

Norway
National Employment Service:
– Arbeidesdirektoratet, Holbergs Plas 7, Postboks 8127 Dep, Oslo 1. Tel: 01 11 10 70.

Portugal
National Employment Service:
– Ministério de Trabalho, Praça de Londres, 1091 Lisbon Codex.

Spain
National Employment Service:
– CNC, General Pardinas 5, Madrid.

Sweden
National Employment Service:
– Arbetmarknadsstryrelsen, Box 2021, 12612 Stockholm

United Kingdom
   National Employment Service:
   – Job Centres. (In most towns.)

WORK PERMITS

Getting a work permit

If you are a citizen of an EU country you do not need a work permit in order to look for or get a job in any other EU country. You are legally entitled to look for a job and carry it out without any permits or visas.

If you wish to stay in the EU country for a period in excess of three months you must obtain a residence permit, whether working or not. This can be obtained from the local police or town hall.

If you are not a citizen of an EU country you will normally require a work permit to work in any of the EU countries. Check with the embassy before you leave. Also see Figure 9.

If you are an EU citizen wishing to work in a non-EU European country you will normally require a work visa and a permit. This must usually be obtained before leaving the country concerned. See Figure 9.

ESSENTIAL DO'S AND DON'TS

Here are some essential points to consider when looking for and taking up a job:

● Illegal working is common in many countries (casual work without a work permit). This is illegal and can result in you being fined, deported or even imprisoned.

● Always make sure you have clearly agreed the rate of pay before starting – together with any other benefits offered, such as meals and accommodation. If they are not free agree what deductions will be made.

● Ask if any deduction will be made for tax or social security.

● Make sure the employer has employer's liability insurance.

● If you are asked to work in unsafe conditions then it is best to leave.

Country	Work permit details
Albania	Foreign workers rarely permitted.
Austria	No permit required for EU citizens. Others require work permit.
Baltic States	N/A
Belarus	Foreign workers rarely permitted.
Belgium	No permit for EU citizens. Others require permit which is obtained by employer.
Bulgaria	Work permits rarely granted.
Czech Republic	Work permit required before entering country.
Denmark	No permit for EU citizens. Permits rarely granted to others.
Finland	No permit for EU citizens. Others must apply for permit.
France	No permit for EU citizens. Others must apply for permit.
Germany	No permit for EU citizens. Others must apply for permit.
Greece	No permit for EU citizens. Others must apply to Ministry of Labour and be supported by employer.
Hungary	Work permit required. Can be obtained in Hungary.
Ireland	No permit for EU citizens. Others must have permit.
Italy	No permit for EU citizens. Others must have permit.
Luxembourg	No permit for EU citizens. Others must have permit.
Netherlands	No permit for EU citizens. Others must have permit.
Norway	Work permit required. Readily granted for EU citizens.
Poland	Work permit required but rarely issued.
Portugal	No permit for EU citizens. Others must have permit.
Romania	Work permit required. Rarely granted.
Russia	Work permit required. Rarely granted.
Slovak Republic	Work permit required. Rarely granted.
Spain	No permit for EU citizens. Others must have permit.
Switzerland	Work permit required. Employer must obtain permit before offering job.
Ukraine	Work permit required. Rarely granted.
United Kingdom	No permit for EU citizens. Others must have one. Citizens of other Commonwealth countries aged 17–27 are more readily granted a permit than others.

Fig. 9. Work permit requirements.

Health and safety regulations are strict in some European countries, but very lax in others.

● Women should be cautious if offered jobs in bars or clubs, especially as hostesses or dancers. These could be genuine but may be a cover for prostitution.

● Everyone should be cautious about being offered jobs as couriers or messengers. This could be a cover for smuggling, especially drug smuggling.

6
Your Guide to Every European Country

ALBANIA

An overview of Albania
Until recently **Albania** was almost completely cut off from the west. Now it has tentatively opened its doors and does accept tourists from abroad. Most travellers report a visit worthwhile to experience the distinctly different way of life but there is not a great deal of tourist interest.

Travel tips
Travel by air from Italy or Hungary, sea from Brindisi or Corfu, or enter by road at Kaklavia on the border with Greece. Public transport is good throughout the country.

Accommodation tips
There are plenty of hotels although these tend to be expensive. Many travellers can see all they want to see on a day trip.

Entry requirements
UK citizens together with most other EU, US and Canadian citizens do not need a visa. Australians do and this should be obtained in advance.

Things to see and do
The capital **Tirana** is a rather bland, modern city. **Shkodra** and **Kruja** are more historic. **Durres** is an industrial town but also Albania's seaside resort.

Don't miss this!
Concerts, opera and theatre in and around the Palace of Culture, free or very cheap.

AUSTRIA

An overview of Austria
Austria is an efficient and tidy country, and a good early or late season call if you'd like to ski. It can also be quite expensive to visit. However, since it is now a member of the EU backpackers are at least allowed to work if they wish to supplement their funds.

Travel tips
Austria is easy to travel to, and around, but not cheap. Train and bus fares are roughly equal. Good for cyclists (apart from the mountains!) and you can rent bikes at most stations.

Accommodation tips
Hotels are expensive. Hostels and camping are a budget alternative but by no means cheap. Staying in private rooms (look for the sign, '**Zimmerfrei**') is a good way of staying on a tight budget.

Useful contacts
The following contacts will be able to advise you on travel and accommodation:

Austrian Foreign Students Service, Rooseveltplatz 13, 1090 Vienna. OKISTA, Garnisongasse 7, 1090 Vienna.

Entry requirements
Citizens of other EU countries do not need a visa or work permit. Citizens of US/Canada/Australia/New Zealand do not require a visa to enter but they may not work.

Things to see and do
Vienna and **Salzburg**, museums, historic buildings, skiing.

Don't miss this!
Stephansdol cathedral and the surrounding streets, rich in Baroque atmosphere. The world-famous Spanish Riding School (closed July and August).

BALTIC STATES

An overview of the Baltic States
The **Baltic States** are a new arrival on the traveller's trail, having

previously been locked away behind the Iron Curtain. They already have a distinct identity from the rest of the former Soviet Union. Indeed, each Baltic country – **Estonia**, **Latvia** and **Lithuania** – has its own identity. Each state is mainly for the more adventurous traveller, although Estonia is probably more 'westernised' than the others.

Travel tips
Other than flying or travelling overland from St Petersburg the best and cheapest way into the Baltic States is from Helsinki to Tallinn by ferry. Public transport is cheap but slow.

Accommodation tips
It is easy enough to find a hotel in the capital cities of **Tallinn**, **Riga** and **Vilnius** and camp sites are available in the suburbs in summer.

Entry requirements
Visas are not required by citizens of EU countries. Others should check before travelling.

Things to see and do
City tours, well-preserved medieval buildings (especially Vilnius, Riga and Tallinn), music and theatre, surprisingly good (and cheap) food, drink and shopping.

Don't miss this!
Interesting food, a combination of Baltic, Polish and Finnish styles!

BELARUS

An overview of Belarus
Belarus is a rarely-visited country of the former Soviet Union. Mostly regarded as a stop-off on the route to Russia it does have an interesting character of its own, with friendly and hospitable people.

Travel tips
You can fly from many European cities but most backpackers arrive on the Berlin–Warsaw–Minsk–Moscow train. Distances in Belarus are longer than you think!

Accommodation tips
Hotels are reasonably inexpensive.

Entry requirements
Most visitors require a visa which is best obtained before arrival.

Things to see and do
Minsk is a modern city, largely rebuilt after World War Two. Traditional music and theatre are on offer. Good café-scene developing.

Don't miss this!
Interesting stop-off to see the way of life but nothing special to report.

BELGIUM

An overview of Belgium
Belgium is very much a multi national country and one where people from all over Europe tend to converge. If you don't find anything to interest you in Belgium itself it's also an excellent point from which to travel to the surrounding countries.

Travel tips
Train travel is extensive, reliable and quite cheap. Belgium is excellent for cycling and recommended for hitchhikers (but not on motorways, of which there are many).

Accommodation tips
Hotels are expensive, and most campsites tend to be costly, luxury establishments. Private rooms are more reasonable. Plenty of IYHF hostels but must book in advance in summer. Unofficial youth hostels (sleep-ins) are basic but very cheap and operate in some cities in summer.

Useful contact
CNIJ, 10 Rue Jean Volders, 1060 Brussels can advise on travel, accommodation and what's on.

Entry requirements
Citizens of most western countries do not need a visa. EU citizens may work in Belgium without a permit.

Things to see and do
Brussels for its cosmopolitan atmosphere, **Antwerp** for culture and nightlife, **Bruges** and **Ghent** for history.

Don't miss this!
Good value food and drink! Interesting palaces and museums in Brussels. Take a look at the EU's famous Berlaymont building which you've seen so many times on TV!

BULGARIA

An overview of Bulgaria
Once a staunchly communist state **Bulgaria** has opened up fast, hoping to attract as many foreign tourists as possible. Most of the cities are modern and lack character but the mountains are breathtaking and the beaches on the Black Sea equal or better those in most Mediterranean countries.

Travel tips
Package tours are good value. Rail travel to Bulgaria can be costly and time-consuming.

Accommodation tips
Hotels, hostels, private rooms and camping are available. Many camp sites on the Black Sea have inexpensive chalets to rent.

Useful contact
Orbita, Boulevard Stamboliski 45, Sofia.

Entry requirements
Visas needed for tourists if not travelling as part of a group tour or package holiday.

Things to see and do
Mountain scenery, good beaches, reasonably cheap food and drink, good and cheap skiing in winter.

Don't miss this!
Golden Sands, Sunny Beach and **Albena** beach resorts. Very cheap if getting a little run down.

CZECH REPUBLIC

An overview of the Czech Republic
Prague itself is one of Europe's most beautiful and well-preserved

cities. No wonder it is now attracting so many tourists. It is fast becoming one of the backpacking capitals of Europe, offering a chance to meet people from all over the world. It is now extremely crowded in summer.

Travel tips
Easy to reach by train from all over Europe. Also good coach services, especially from Vienna.

Accommodation tips
Hotels are becoming expensive. Cheap camping, youth hostels and private rooms are available but it can be hard to find accommodation in the height of summer.

Useful contact
CKM (Czech Youth and Student Travel Bureau), Zitna Ulice 12, 12105 Prague.

Entry requirements
EU citizens do not need a visa for a stay of less than a month. Other nationalities should check first.

Things to see and do
Superb architecture especially in **Prague** and very good social scene too. Good theatre, music, shopping and food. Try the thermal spas!

Don't miss this!
Prague, city of a hundred spires including the world-famous Astronomical clock and St Nicholas church.

DENMARK

An overview of Denmark
Denmark is an attractive partly-island nation with hospitable people. **Copenhagen** is a fascinating city which is very busy in summer and a good place from which to continue your journey to Norway or Sweden.

Travel tips
Buses are reasonably priced. Train travel can be expensive (more costly during the week). Excellent for cycling.

Accommodation tips

Hotels are very expensive. Private rooms are plentiful and there are also many, reasonably-priced youth hostels. For really basic, budget accommodation look for a 'sleep-in' – basic dormitory or community centre accommodation which operates during the summer.

Useful contact
Denmark Internationale Studenterkomite, Skindergade 36,
   Copenhagen.

Entry requirements

EU citizens and citizens of most other western countries do not need a visa for a tourist stay. EU citizens may work without a permit.

Things to see and do

Danish island-hopping, cycling, good fishing. Great café society and social life in Copenhagen (but not cheap).

Don't miss this!

World famous **Tivoli** pleasure gardens in **Copenhagen**.

FINLAND

An overview of Finland

Finland comprises thousands of lakes and forests and **Helsinki** is the only large city. It makes a good springboard for a trip to **St Petersburg**, or up into **Lapland**.

Travel tips

Expensive to travel to and within **Finland**. Rail travel expensive so Inter Rail is a good option. Hitchhiking recommended.

Accommodation tips

Expensive hotels. Good youth hostels but book ahead in summer. Reasonably-priced student hotels operate in summer in university accommodation.

Useful contacts
Kompassi, Simonkatu 1, 00100 Helsinki. Tel: 612 1863.

SRM Travel, Yrjökatu 38 B15, 00100 Helsinki. Tel: 694 0377.

(Discount on flights, rail travel, car hire *etc.*)

Entry requirements
EU citizens don't need a visa or work permit. Citizens of other western countries do not normally require a visa for a tourist stay but may not work.

Things to see and do
Hiking, fishing, boating, good museums.

Don't miss this!
A trip to **Lapland** in the far north if you get the chance!

Case history
Paul Jones and two friends decided to backpack around Scandinavia last summer:

'We didn't want to follow the usual backpacker's trails so we decided to head for Denmark, Sweden and Finland. People say that Scandinavia is expensive, and it does live up to its reputation, but if you spend carefully it can be done. Hotels were completely out, even the cheap ones. We used quite a few youth hostels and found private rooms fairly affordable. Food is fairly costly too. Buying Inter Rail passes made our trip affordable and apart from that we spent hardly anything on transport. Copenhagen is great in summer and it was worth the trip up in the Arctic Circle, just so we can say that we've been!'

FRANCE

An overview of France
France is the ideal country for backpacking. There's so much to see all in the one country, and facilities for travellers are generally very good. France is also a very good base for side-trips to neighbouring countries, especially Germany, Switzerland and Italy.

Travel tips
Excellent network of trains, especially north–south. A supplement is payable over the price of your Inter Rail pass if you want to try travel on the ultra-fast TGV. Good for cyclists and recommended for hitching.

Accommodation tips

France has an abundance of cheap accommodation, including hotels, hostels and inns. You can always get a list from the local tourist information office. Good for camping, but can be expensive in summer. Try to book at least a night ahead in July and August (especially in the south) when accommodation is at a premium.

Useful contact
Fédération Unie des Auberges de Jeunesse, 27 rue Pajol, 75018 Paris. Tel: 1 46 07 00 01.

Entry requirements

EU citizens don't need a visa and can work without a work permit. Citizens of most other western countries do not need a visa for a tourist stay but are not usually allowed to work.

Things to see and do

Great beaches, social life, sports, cultural sites, music, concerts, food and wine.

Don't miss this!

Paris should be on every backpacker's trip. The **Côte d'Azur** is also well worth a visit.

GERMANY

An overview of Germany

Germany is famous as the land of efficiency, which makes it a particularly easy country to travel around, if not particularly cheap. Many travellers find much of western Germany rather sterile – the former eastern Germany is much more interesting, though travel is by no means as streamlined, nor facilities as good.

Travel tips

Trains are good (in the west) but expensive so your Inter Rail pass will earn its keep. Buses are good and rail passes can be used on some coaches. Hitching is usually easy and cyclists are well catered for.

Accommodation tips

Hotels are expensive and, in cities, often booked up especially when there is a trade fair which is a frequent event in many of them. Guest houses (*Gasthauser*) and private rooms (*Zimmer Frei*) are more reasonable. Youth hostels are good but you often need to book to be sure of a bed.

Useful contacts

Deutsches Jugendherbergswerk, Hauptverband, Bismarckstrasse 8, Postfach 1455, 4930 Detmold. (German Youth Hostel Association.)

Youth Information Centre, Paul Heysestrasse 22, 80336. Munich. (Gives help and advice on travel and accommodation for young people.)

Entry requirements

EU citizens don't need a visa and can work without a work permit. Citizens of other western countries don't normally need a visa but may not work.

Things to see and do

Medieval towns, cities little changed since the war (eastern Germany), the **Black Forest**, the **Alps**, the **Rhineland**, beer festivals.

Don't miss this!

Berlin, Munich, Cologne, Dresden.

GREECE

An overview of Greece

Greece and the **Greek Islands** are something of a paradise for backpackers. Travel, food and accommodation are cheap and there is something for everyone from lovers of culture to lovers of nightclubs. Most places, however, are jam-packed during the summer and you mustn't underestimate the cost and distance of Greece from the UK and Ireland.

Travel tips

A cheap package holiday or cheap flight may be more cost-effective than train or coach. Local trains and buses are cheap, but often run to uncertain timetables. Island-hopping by ferry is fun and cheap but plan your journey carefully as most ferries run to and from Piraeus (port of Athens) rather than from island to island.

Accommodation tips
It's normally easy to find a cheap place to stay in Greece. Small pensions and rooms in private houses offer the best bargains and you don't normally need to book.

Entry requirements
EU citizens and citizens of most western countries do not need a visa.

Things to see and do
Historic sites, museums, folklore shows, great beaches and scenery, fabulous nightlife and watersports in resorts, inexpensive food and drink.

Don't miss this!
Athens (despite being hot and overcrowded in summer), the **Parthenon**, the **Greek Isles**, real Greek food in an out-of-the-way (non-tourist) restaurant.

Case history
Fiona King spent three weeks 'island hopping' around the Greek Isles in July and August.

'Island hopping is as good as they say. We're both glad that we decided to go. Once you get to Athens there's a vast choice of islands with tempting names you can choose from and it's still fairly cheap to get there and to stay once you arrive, although the touristy ones are more expensive than the others. We enjoyed a bit of everything – sun, sand, beaches and some culture too! My advice to anyone thinking of doing the same would be to plan before you go – we didn't, which looking back wasn't a good idea because we only just made it back to Athens at the end of the stay. By the way, don't expect the ferries to fit in with your plans – they run to a laid-back, "we'll get-there-when-we-get-there" Greek timetable which can be maddening at times.'

HUNGARY

An overview of Hungary
For an eastern European country **Hungary** is now quite westernised in some ways, but still retains at least some of its time-stood-still character. **Budapest** is a historic city, but you can also visit the resorts on **Lake Balaton** or take a trip on the **Danube**.

Travel tips
Other than flying, train is the quickest way of reaching Hungary. The best route is via **Vienna**. There are also coach services from most European capitals.

Trains are good but buses offer a cheaper and generally more reliable method of transport. Hitching is possible but not easy.

Accommodation tips
There are plenty of reasonably-priced hotels. Private rooms offer a bargain-priced option. There are several youth hostels, and universities in major towns rent out their accommodation during the summer.

Useful contact
BITEJ (International Bureau for Youth Tourism and Exchange), Ady E Utca, 1024 Budapest.

Entry requirements
EU and US citizens do not need a visa for a tourist stay. Others should check the current requirements.

Things to see and do
Budapest, the famous Castle Hill, a Danube trip, fashionable social scene in Budapest. **Pecs** and **Szeged** are interesting and fashionable regional towns.

Don't miss this!
Outdoor thermal baths, for which Hungary is famous. Good and reasonably priced food and beer.

IRELAND

An overview of Ireland
Ireland is a more off-the-beaten track destination for backpackers looking for a slower pace of life. However, **Dublin** offers a surprisingly cosmopolitan way of life. Don't come for the weather.

Travel tips
Easy and cheap to reach by ferry from the UK. Also bargain-priced flight deals available from many UK cities. Trains are reasonably

efficient but expensive, buses are slower but reasonably priced. Hitching is usually easy in rural areas.

Accommodation tips
No shortage of inexpensive bed and breakfast accommodation and youth hostels.

Useful contacts
Community and Youth Information Centre, Sackville House, Sackville Place, Dublin 1. Tel: 1 878 6844.

Irish Youth Hostel Association, Travel Section, 39 Mountjoy Square, Dublin 1. Tel: 01 363 111.

Entry requirements
EU citizens do not need a visa or a work permit and British citizens do not even require a passport. Nationals of most western countries do not require a visa for a tourist stay and US and Canadian students can obtain a working holiday visa if they wish to work.

Things to see and do
Dublin, Cork, the west coast, Irish pubs, fishing, camping, hiking, music, concerts, very fashionable social scene in Dublin.

Don't miss this!
Irish pubs, **Guinness!**

ITALY

An overview of Italy
Italy offers something for every kind of traveller, from those looking for a taste of culture, to those looking for a lively social scene. It is also a country of many contrasts with the sharpest being between the prosperous north and less wealthy south. Overall, Italy is a destination which should not be missed although it is not always an easy option for the budget backpacker.

Travel tips
Italy is easy to reach by train and long-distance coaches operate from most large European cities. Within Italy trains are reliable and really quite cheap. Buses are cheap but run to unreliable schedules. Hitching is possible, especially in the north, but take the usual precautions.

Accommodation tips

Hotels are expensive but guest houses (*locandas*) or inns (*pensioni*) are good value, and sometimes as cheap as youth hostels. You'll find that campsites are often luxury-type establishments and quite expensive. The well-used Italian '*albergo diurno*' provide a daytime wash-and-brush-up facility, ideal for travellers.

Useful contact
Youth and Student Travel Service, Via Zanetti 18, 50123 Florence.

Entry requirements

EU citizens don't need a visa or work permit. Other nationalities do not normally need a visa to visit as tourists.

Things to see and do

Rome, Florence, Venice, Naples, Sorrento, the **Italian Lakes,** Italian food and wine, the social life, taking an evening stroll through town.

Don't miss this!

Venice and the Vatican City are must-see destinations for all travellers!

LUXEMBOURG

An overview of Luxembourg

As a relatively small country **Luxembourg** is not a place you are likely to stay for long. However, it does offer good connections to surrounding countries and has an interesting multinational atmosphere.

Travel tips

Easy to travel to and through by rail and bus.

Accommodation tips

Budget-priced accommodation can be hard to find. Better to stay in either Belgium or France.

Things to see and do

Luxembourg town, EU institutions.

Don't miss this!

Nothing particularly to recommend.

NETHERLANDS

An overview of the Netherlands

Amsterdam is another one of those cities which seems to attract backpackers by the thousand, especially during the summer. It offers interesting surroundings, culture, history and the liberal-minded attitude towards drugs for which it has become world famous. It is also an excellent place to pick up cheap travel to other European cities. Bear in mind that outside Amsterdam and the larger cities attitudes are less liberal, but you will find an abundance of bulbfields, dykes and areas reclaimed from the sea for which the Netherlands is equally well-known.

Travel tips

Excellent, comprehensive and reasonably-priced bus and train services. Ideal for cyclists. Recommended for hitchhiking and some towns even boast special hitchhikers 'pick up' stops on the outskirts!

Accommodation tips

Plenty of inexpensive small hotels in most areas. Private rooms good value. Almost 50 IYHF hostels throughout the country. In summer you will also find 'sleep-in' dormitories in the main towns which offer basic accommodation but which are very cheap.

Useful contacts

NBBS Travel has information centres in most cities and towns.

Entry requirements

EU citizens don't need a visa to visit the Netherlands, nor a work permit if wishing to work. Nationals of the US, Canada, Australia and New Zealand do not need a visa but are not normally allowed to work.

Things to see and do

Canals, social life, cycling, boating, Dutch beer. **Leiden, Delft** and the **Hague** (for those in search of history).

Don't miss this!

Amsterdam, a must for every backpacking trip.

NORWAY

An overview of Norway

There's nowhere on earth quite like **Norway**, being a country of mountains and fjords that are every bit as spectacular as they look on TV. Norway shares little in common with most of the rest of Europe (it isn't even a member of the EU). Norway can be an expensive country in which to travel and stay.

Travel tips

Flying is the easiest way to Norway and there are a few bargains to be had from discount agencies. The rail network is limited but good, and also rather expensive. Your Inter Rail card will come in handy! You'll need to use a ferry to reach many places and these are good value.

Accommodation tips

Hotels are very expensive. Private rooms are a cheaper option. There are plenty of youth hostels but it's best to book in summer. Camping is a good option in summer and, as well as the many organised sites, it's legal to camp rough anywhere!

Useful contact
Norwegian Student Travel Office, PO Box 55, Oslo 3.

Entry requirements

Citizens of most western countries can visit as tourists without a visa. EU nationals may work in Norway, even though Norway is not a member of the EU.

Things to see and do

Oslo, Bergen, Nordkapp, fjord trips, hiking.

Don't miss this!

A trip on the **Hurtigrute** ferry along the coast and up into the **Arctic Circle** (but unfortunately it's not cheap).

POLAND

An overview of Poland

Poland probably won't ever attract many backpackers, although it is generally an underrated destination for travellers. **Warsaw** is a historic city, which still retains some of the mystique of the Iron Curtain days and rural Poland offers some attractive scenery and friendly people. It's also still quite cheap.

Travel tips
Poland is easily reached by rail and coach from most European cities. Local trains and buses are good and cheap. Hitchhiking is positively encouraged through the official **Autostop scheme**.

Accommodation tips
Hotels are inexpensive (apart from the luxury ones) but the cheapest can be very basic. Rooms in private homes are incredibly cheap but, again, usually quite basic. You can get details at tourist offices or look for signs saying *'Pokoje'*. There are plenty of youth hostels but they are busy in summer.

Useful contacts
Almatur, U1. Kopernike 15, 00364 Warsaw.
Polskie Towarzystwo Schronisk, Mlodziezowych, U1. Chocimska 28, 00791 Warsaw.

Entry requirements
Most visitors can stay as tourists for up to 90 days (UK citizens six months) without a visa.

Things to see and do
Museums, concerts, fishing, hiking, most sports, food and drink (especially vodka) at very reasonable prices.

Don't miss this!
Krakow, the ancient capital.

PORTUGAL

An overview of Portugal
Portugal is a good destination for the budget traveller – it's unhurried, uncrowded and friendly. You'll still find places where being a foreigner is considered a novelty. It's still incredibly cheap to travel and stay in Portugal, though more expensive in the main tourist areas of **Lisbon** and the **Algarve.**

Travel tips

You can travel by train to Portugal but a cheap flight or using a package holiday may work out cheaper. Local trains and buses are cheap but not always fast or reliable. Hitching is difficult as traffic volumes are low in most places.

Accommodation tips

You should always be able to find an inexpensive hotel, pension or private room accommodation – but it is wise to book ahead in the Algarve in July and August. Youth hostels are fairly few.

Useful contact

Turicoop, Rua Pascal de Melo 15–1, 1100 Lisbon. Will arrange budget accommodation for young people.

Entry requirements

EU citizens and those of most western countries do not need a visa. EU citizens may work without a permit.

Things to see and do

Fabulous beaches (usually uncrowded), watersports, tennis and golf, museums and historic sites (often free or at very little cost), food and drink at very reasonable prices, good nightlife in resorts.

Don't miss this!

Lisbon and **Oporto** for lovers of culture. **Albufeira** and **Praia da Rocha** for beach lovers!

ROMANIA

An overview of Romania

Romania doesn't appear on the itinerary of many backpackers. It does have a reputation of being a rather run-down, unloved country but it does have lovely countryside, interesting architecture and friendly people.

Travel tips

Travel to Romania can be expensive, especially by air. Even the rail journey can be costly with poor connections to most European cities. Internally, train is the only reliable method of transport so plan journeys carefully.

Accommodation tips

Most hotel accommodation is of a poor standard and not always cheap. It's also possible to stay in private rooms.

Entry requirements

All nationalities need a visa which takes seven days to obtain and lasts for three months.

Things to see and do

Bucharest, Transylvania, quite good skiing in winter.

Don't miss this!

Nothing particular to recommend.

RUSSIA

An overview of Russia

Russia is mainly a destination for the very adventurous traveller. Even then, you would need to plan carefully to go very far: **Moscow** and **St Petersburg** are reasonably accessible to backpackers. Elsewhere distances are vast and transport services are unreliable.

Travel tips

It is not cheap to travel to Russia. There are youth fares to Moscow and some of the eastern European airlines have flight bargains, via their own capital city, if your travel agent can arrange them. There are direct trains from most European capitals to Moscow.

Accommodation tips

Russian hotels are often of poor quality (except luxury establishments), and not cheap. It is possible to stay in private houses and apartments. A new Russian Youth Hostels Association is opening up hostels throughout Russia. There are already hostels in Moscow and St Petersburg which can also be booked through the YHA Travel Shop, 14 Southampton Street, London WC2E 7HY.

Useful contact
Russian Youth Hostels, 3rd Sovetskaya Street 28, St Petersburg 193312. Russia.

Entry requirements
Visas are required for most nationalities. This takes at least two weeks and they should be obtained before leaving home.

Things to see and do
Historic buildings and sites, museums, theatre, concerts, opera, ballet, circus, most sports, much improved food and drink, increasingly lively social scene in Moscow and St Petersburg.

Don't miss this!
Red Square and the **Kremlin** in **Moscow, St Petersburg**.

SLOVAK REPUBLIC

An overview of the Slovak Republic
The **Slovak Republic** was formed in 1993 after the division of **Czechoslovakia**. It is quieter and more rural than its brasher, more cosmopolitan neighbour and not on the itinerary of many backpackers.

Travel tips
Easy to reach by train or bus via **Vienna** or **Prague.**

Accommodation tips
Inexpensive but poor quality hotels. Private rooms are now available, a few youth hostels and many sites.

Useful contact
Slovak Academic Information Agency, Hviezdoslavovo Namesti 14, 21429 Bratislava.

Entry requirements
Citizens of most western countries don't need a visa for a short tourist stay.

Things to see and do
The **Old Quarter of Bratislava** is unspoiled and historic. The **Tatra Mountains** are good for camping and hiking.

Don't miss this!
Nothing particular to recommend.

SPAIN

An overview of Spain
Spain is more usually regarded as a destination for package holiday-makers. In fact, if you're looking for beaches and good nightlife you'll find it hard to backpack much cheaper than the cheapest two week package. If you want to see the real Spain, however, backpacking is the ideal way of doing it cheaply.

Travel tips
Look for a cheap flight. Alternatively travel through France by rail, for which it's worth having an Inter Rail pass. Spanish trains are reasonably priced but the network is complicated. Plan ahead. Many rail tickets can be used on rail buses. Hitchhiking is not easy.

Accommodation tips
There is no shortage of reasonably-priced hotels, pensions, guesthouses and private rooms in Spain. You don't normally need to book. Youth hostels are rare. It is legal to camp rough, but not on beaches.

Useful contact
Oficina Nacional de Intercambio y Turismo de Jovenes y Estudiantes (TIVE), José Ortega y Gasset 71, 28006 Madrid.

Entry requirements
EU citizens don't need a visa and can work without a work permit. Nationals of most other western countries do not need a visa for a tourist stay.

Things to see and do
Good beaches, wide choice of sports and watersports, good nightlife in resorts. Inexpensive food and drink. Plenty of cultural sites in cities such as **Seville, Toledo** and **Granada**.

Don't miss this!
Marbella, for a taste of the high life. The **Alhambra** at Granada for lovers of history who want to see something of the real Spain.

Case history
Ian Riley travelled along the Spanish Costas in March and April:

'I'd been to Majorca on a package holiday before and couldn't believe how different the real Spain is. Away from the resorts the local people are much friendlier and prices of food, accommodation *etc* so much less. Really it's like a different country. On the minus side, distances are longer than I expected and in between the towns and resorts there really isn't a lot for tourists to see and do.'

SWEDEN

An overview of Sweden
Sweden is one of the more expensive European cities in which to stay and care is needed when travelling on a budget. Nevertheless if you want to visit Scandinavia it makes a good choice and **Stockholm** is a beautiful clean, green city-on-the-water.

Travel tips
Swedish trains are excellent but expensive. It's well worth having some form of discount pass. Bus services are good and slightly cheaper. Hitchhiking is not usually successful.

Accommodation tips
Hotels are cheaper than elsewhere in Scandinavia but you'll need to shop around to find a bargain. There are plenty of youth hostels, but book ahead in summer. Camp sites are plentiful too and many have cabins for rent which work out fairly inexpensive for groups.

Useful contact
SFS Resebyra, Kungsgaten 4, PO Box 7144, 10387 Stockholm.

Entry requirements
Most nationalities do not need a visa for a tourist stay. EU nationals may work without a work permit.

Things to see and do
Fishing, boating, hiking, camping, good social life in **Stockholm** (but can be expensive). Stockholm is ideal for exploring on foot. You could also visit the **Arctic Circle** by train.

Don't miss this!
Old Stockholm, the island of **Gotland** in summer.

SWITZERLAND

An overview of Switzerland
Switzerland is a scenic and beautiful country and well worth a short trip. In fact, your trip may be short by necessity as Switzerland is incredibly expensive too. If you're careful, however, backpacking is the cheapest way you're likely to find of exploring the country. Ideal for skiers but worth visiting in summer too.

Travel tips
Easy to reach by train or coach from most European capitals. Trains are excellent but expensive and you can use your Inter Rail pass on most of the trunk routes but *not* on many branch line services. Postbuses offer inexpensive local transport in the most mountainous areas. Hitching is possible but not easy and cycling largely impractical due to the geography!

Accommodation tips
Plan carefully as hotels, guest houses and even private rooms can be very expensive. Youth hostels are the main choice for budget travellers but you should book ahead in summer. Camping is possible, but many sites are open in the peak season only.

Useful contact
Swiss Student Travel Office (SSR Reisen), Backerstrasse 4c, 8026 Zurich.

Entry requirements
Nationals of most countries do not need a visa for a tourist stay. However, everyone wishing to work in Switzerland requires a combined work/residence permit which is issued by the employer.

Things to see and do
Zurich, Geneva, Lausanne, Montreux, Interlaken, the **Lakes,** the Alpine ski resorts, the **Matterhorn.**

Don't miss this!
A trip on **Lake Geneva** and any of the swish resorts along its shore.

Case history
Victoria Vasey and two friends spent a week in Switzerland before spending the rest of their month away in France.

'Switzerland is a stunning country, so green and clean that it makes everywhere else look shabby. Yes it is expensive but as long as you stay away from posh looking hotels and restaurants and don't want to sit in smart cafés all day sipping coffee it's not too difficult to get by. We definitely want to go back and at the moment we are thinking of going back on a working trip and trying to find a job in a hotel or as chalet maids.'

UKRAINE

An overview of Ukraine
The **Ukraine** is the second largest state, in population terms, to have emerged from the Soviet Union. **Kiev,** the capital, is a surprisingly elegant city which is striving to regain some of the grandeur of the days prior to the formation of the USSR. The countryside is fertile agricultural land – called the 'garden of the Soviet Union' – apart from the radiation zone around the Chernobyl nuclear reactor which exploded in 1986.

Travel tips
It is difficult and expensive to fly to Kiev, except from Moscow. Regular trains leave from **Prague, Budapest** and **Moscow.**

Accommodation tips
There are inexpensive but basic hotels and private rooms available and there are campsites on the outskirts of Kiev. No hostels exist at present, but this is likely to change.

Entry requirements
All foreign visitors require a visa. This takes up ten days from a Ukraine embassy or consulate and is valid for 90 days.

Things to do and see
Kiev has plenty of historic (and not so historic) public buildings and museums, good theatres and concerts and reasonably good shopping. Ukrainian food and drink is some of the best in the former USSR.

Don't miss this!
The old part of Kiev, including **St Sophia's Cathedral** is interesting, and you may get a chance to watch **Dynamo Kiev!**

UNITED KINGDOM

An overview of the UK
The **UK** should certainly be on the itinerary of all travellers from overseas offering as it does something for everyone. Whilst you'll probably want to base yourself in **London** also try to visit some of the regions and, if possible, Scotland and Wales which each have their own distinct identities.

Travel tips
Cheap flights can be had from most European cities by shopping around. Try flying into a regional city rather than London which is often much cheaper. You can now travel direct by Eurostar train from Paris or Brussels. For internal travel coaches are reasonably priced. Long-distance rail travel is expensive unless you have some kind of pass.

Accommodation tips
Hotels can be expensive but often have very cheap special offers at weekends. There is no shortage of small hotels, bed and breakfast guesthouses and pubs offering accommodation in most places. There are many youth hostels but you must book ahead in summer in the major tourist areas.

Useful contacts
Scottish Youth Hostels Association, 7 Glebe Crescent, Stirling FK8
    2JA. Tel: (01786) 51181.
Youth Hostels Association (England and Wales), 8 St Stephen's Hill,
    St Albans, Herts AL1 2DY. Tel: (01727) 55215.

Entry requirements
EU citizens do not need a visa and can work without a work permit. Citizens of the USA and many Commonwealth countries do not need a visa for a tourist stay but may not work. Citizens of some Commonwealth countries (including Canada, Australia and New Zealand) aged 17–27 may take a working holiday in the UK for up to two years. Check with your nearest British embassy or consulate.

Things to see and do
Cities such as **London, Oxford, Cambridge, York, Edinburgh** and **Chester** offer an almost unlimited choice of historic buildings, sites and

other attractions of interest to tourists. Coastal resorts are popular in summer. Most large towns and cities have a wide range of theatres, concerts, sporting activities and busy nightlife.

Don't miss this!

In London, **Buckingham Palace** (open to the public in summer), **Westminster Abbey**, the **Tower of London** and the many museums are regarded as 'must sees' by travellers from abroad.

SUMMARY

Ten more tips to make your trip a success

1.   Set a departure date to aim for.

2.   Make sure everybody contributes to your itinerary.

3.   Get estimates of likely travel costs *as soon as* you have decided where you wish to go.

4.   Do your homework. Read up on preferred destinations and if you can talk to people who've been there.

5.   If there's something you've always wanted to see then plan your trip around that.

6.   Be realistic. Don't overstretch your budget or the time you have available.

7.   If your budget is really tight cut a few days off your trip. It's easier than trying to do without meals, proper accommodation *etc.*

8.   If you're hoping to work as you go to pay for your trip remember that it can be *very* hard to find jobs (because everyone else is trying to do the same thing).

9.   Avoid last minute changes if possible.

10. Always have an **emergency fund** to pay for your trip home if something goes wrong. And always take insurance!

Planning chart

Use this chart to start making plans for your trip:

● Likely departure date:

● Likely return date:

● Number of people travelling:

● Countries you wish to visit:

● Places you wish to visit:

● Main method of travel:

● Approximate amount you have to spend:

  ● On travel:

  ● On accommodation:

  ● On food:

  ● On entertainment:

● Do you wish to work?

● If so, where and doing what?

● Passport required?

● Visas required?

● Main items of clothing/equipment to buy/borrow:

Keeping a log
Whilst on your trip it is useful to keep detailed records of where you've been, how far you've travelled each day, what the weather was like and any other comments. As you will undoubtedly be packing this book in your backpack Figure 10 provides you with a backpackers log on which to record all this information.

Backpackers' log

Date:	Journey:	Distance from/to (Km):	Weather:	Comments:

Fig. 10. Backpackers' Log.

Date:	Journey:	Distance from/to (Km):	Weather:	Comments:

Date:	Journey:	Distance from/to (Km):	Weather:	Comments:

TOURIST OFFICES/BOARDS IN LONDON

Austria
30 St George Street, London W1R 0AL. Tel: (0171) 629 0461.

Belgium
29 Princes Street, London W1R 7RG. Tel: (0171) 629 0230.

Bulgaria
18 Princes Street, London W1R 7TE. Tel: (0171) 499 6988.

Czech Republic
49 Southwark Street, London SE1 1RU. Tel: (0171) 378 6009.

Denmark
55 Sloane Street, London SW1X 9SR. Tel: (0171) 259 5959.

Finland
66 Haymarket, London SW1Y 4RF. Tel: (0171) 839 4048.

France
178 Piccadilly, London W1V 0AL. Tel: 0891 244123.

Germany
65 Curzon Street, London W1Y 7PE. Tel: 0891 600100.

Greece
4 Conduit Street, London W1R 0DJ. Tel: (0171) 734 5997.

Hungary
PO Box 4336, London SW18 4XE. Tel: (0181) 871 4009.

Ireland
150 New Bond Street, London W1Y 0AQ. Tel: (0171) 493 3201.

Italy
1 Princes Street, London W1R 8AY. Tel: (0171) 408 1254.

Luxembourg
122 Regent Street, London W1R 5FE. Tel: (0171) 434 2800.

Netherlands
PO Box 253, London SW1E 6NT. Tel: 0891 200277.

Norway
5–11 Lower Regent Street, London SW1Y 4LR. Tel: (0171) 839 2650.

Poland
82 Mortimer Street, London W1N 7DE. Tel: (0171) 580 8028.

Portugal
22 Sackville Street, London W1X 1DE. Tel: (0171) 494 1441.

Romania
83 Marylebone High Street, London W1M 3DE. Tel: (0171) 224 3692.

Russia
219 Marsh Wall, London E14 9FG. Tel: (0171) 538 8600.

Slovak Republic
49 Southwark Street, London SE1 1RU. Tel: (0171) 378 6009.

Spain
57–58 St James's Street, London SW1A 1LD. Tel: (0171) 499 0901.

Sweden
72–73 Welbeck Street, London W1M 8AN. Tel: 0891 200280.

Switzerland
Swiss Court, New Coventry Street, London W1V 8EE. Tel: (0171) 734 1921.

EMBASSIES AND CONSULATES

Albania
131 Rue de la Pompe, 75016 Paris, France. Tel: 1 45 53 51 32.

Austria
18 Belgrave Mews West, London SW1X 8HU. Tel: (0171) 235 3731.

Baltic States

Estonia
16 Hyde Park Gate, London SW7 5DG. Tel: (0171) 589 3428.

Latvia
72 Queensborough Terrace, London W2 3SP. Tel: (0171) 727 1698.

Lithuania
17 Essex Villas, London W8 7BP. Tel: (0171) 938 2481.

Belarus
1 St Stephen's Crescent, London W2 5QT. Tel: (0171) 225 4568.

Belgium
103 Eaton Square, London SW1W 9AB. Tel: (0171) 235 5422.

Bulgaria
186 Queen's Gate, London SW7 3HL. Tel: (0171) 584 9400.

Czech Republic
25 Kensington Palace Gardens, London W8 4QX. Tel: (0171) 229 1255.

Denmark
55 Sloane Street, London SW1X 9SR. Tel: (0171) 235 1255.

Finland
38 Chesham Place, London SW1X 8HW. Tel: (0171) 235 9531.

France
58 Knightsbridge, London SW1X 7JT. Tel: (0171) 235 8080.

Germany
23 Belgrave Square, London SW1X 8PZ. Tel: (0171) 235 5033.

Greece
1A Holland Park, London W11 3TP. Tel: (0171) 727 8040.

Hungary
35 Eaton Place, London SW1. Tel: (0171) 235 4048.

Ireland
17 Grosvenor Place, London SW1X 7HR. Tel: (0171) 235 2171.

Italy
14 Three Kings Yard, London W1Y 2EH. Tel: (0171) 629 8200.

Luxembourg
27 Wilton Crescent, London SW1X 8SD. Tel: (0171) 235 6961.

Netherlands
38 Hyde Park Gate, London SW7 5DP. Tel: (0171) 581 5040.

Norway
25 Belgrave Square, London SW1X 8QD. Tel: (0171) 235 7151.

Poland
47 Portland Place, London W1N 3AG. Tel: (0171) 580 4324.

Portugal
62 Brompton Road, London SW3 1BJ. Tel: (0171) 581 8722.

Romania
4 Palace Green, London W8 4QD. Tel: (0171) 937 9666.

Russia
13 Kensington Palace Gardens, London W8 4QX. Tel: (0171) 229 3628.

Slovak Republic
25 Kensington Palace Gardens, London W8 4QY. Tel: (0171) 243 0803.

Spain
24 Belgrave Square, London SW1X 8QA. Tel: (0171) 235 5555.

Sweden
11 Montagu Place, London W1H 2AL. Tel: (0171) 724 2101.

Switzerland
16–18 Montagu Place, London W1H 2BQ. Tel: (0171) 723 0701.

Ukraine
78 Kensington Palace Gardens, London W11 2PL. Tel: (0171) 727 6312.

MISCELLANEOUS USEFUL ADDRESSES

Association of British Travel Agents (ABTA), 55 Newman Street, London W1P 4AH. Tel: (0171) 637 2444.

Automobile Association (AA), Fanum House, Basingstoke, Hants RG21 2EA. Tel: (01256) 20123. For information and assistance for motorists.

Berlitz School of Languages, Wells House, 79 Wells Street, London W1A 3BZ. Tel: (0171) 580 6482. Language classes and courses.

British Airways Immunization Service, 156 Regent Street, London W1. Tel: (0171) 439 9584. No appointment necessary for immunizations. BA Travel Clinics can also be found in 25 other towns. Call (0171) 831 5333 for details of your nearest.

Camping and Caravanning Club, Green Fields House, Westwood Way, Coventry CV4 8SH. Information and advice for campers. Issues Camping Carnets.

Campus Travel, 52 Grosvenor Gardens, London SW1W 0AG. Tel: (0171) 730 3402. Discount travel agency.

Council Travel, 28a Poland Street, London W1V 3DB. Tel: (0171) 287 3337. Discount travel agency.

Department of Health, Public Enquiries Office, Richmond House, 79 Whitehall, London SW1A 2NS. Tel: (0171) 210 4850. Information on health services.

Department of Social Security, Overseas Branch, Newcastle Upon Tyne NE98 1YX. Can provide information on availability of health services in Europe. Call 0800 555777 for leaflets.

Eurolines, 23 Crawley Road, Luton LU1 1HX. Tel: (01582) 404511. Europe-wide coach operator.

HM Customs Advice Centre, Dorset House, Stamford Street, London SE1 9NG. Tel: (0171) 202 4227. Advice on Customs regulations in the UK.

ISIC Mail Order, Bleaklow House, Mill Street, Glossop, Derbyshire SK13 8PT. Tel: (01203) 694995. Issues ISIC discount card.

Linguaphone, St Giles House, 50 Poland Street, London W1V 4AX. Tel: (0171) 734 0574. Provides language courses.

Overseas Jobs Express, Premier House, Shoreham Airport, Sussex BN43 5FF. Tel: (01273) 440220. Newspaper with overseas job vacancy advertisements.

Rapid Visa Service, 131–135 Earls Court Road, London SW5 9RH. Tel: (0171) 373 3026.

Royal Autombile Club (RAC), PO Box 100, RAC House, 7 Brighton Road, South Croydon CR2 6XW. Tel: (0181) 989 0088. Information, advice and assistance for motorists.

Scottish Youth Hostels Association, 7 Glebe Crescent, Stirling FK8 2JA. Tel: (01786) 51181.

STA Travel, 6 Wrights Lane, London W8 6TA. Tel: (0171) 938 4711. Discount travel agency.

Stanfords, 12–14 Long Acre, London WC2 9LP. Tel: (0171) 836 1321. Reputedly the largest map seller in the world. Offers a mail order service.

Thames Consular Services, 363 Chiswick High Road, London W4
4HS. Tel: (0181) 995 2492. Can obtain visas on behalf of travellers.

The Backpacker's Club, PO Box 381, Reading RG3 4RL.

Thomas Cook Passport and Visa Service, 45 Berkeley Street, London
W1A 1EB. Tel: (0171) 408 4141. Can obtain visas on behalf of
travellers.

Trailfinders, 42/50 Earls Court Road, London W8 6EJ. Tel: (0171) 938
3366. Discount travel agency.

Travelmates, 15 Cavendish Road, Bournemouth BH7 7AD. Tel:
(01202) 558314. Introduction service for lone travellers.

WEXAS International, 45–49 Brompton Road, London SW3 1DE.
Tel: (0171) 589 3315. Discount travel services.

Youth Hostels Association (England and Wales), 8 St Stephen's Hill,
St Albans, Herts AL1 2DY. Tel: (01727) 55215.

PASSPORT OFFICES

Clive House, 70–78 Petty France, London SW1H 9HD. Tel: (0171)
279 3434.
Fifth Floor, India Buildings, Water Street, Liverpool L2 0QZ. Tel:
(0151) 237 3010.
Olympia House, Upper Dock Street, Newport, Gwent NP9 1XA. Tel:
(01633) 244500.
Aragon Court, Northminster Road, Peterborough PE1 1QC. Tel:
(01733) 895555.
3 Northgate, 96 Milton Street, Cowcaddens, Glasgow G4 0BT. Tel:
(0141) 332 0271.
Hampton House, 47–53 High Street, Belfast BT1 2QS. Tel: (01232)
232371.

Further Reading

GUIDE BOOKS

Of course, you'll find masses of guide books at any library or
bookshop. In this section we list some of the main series to look out
for and where they cover:

Fodor's Guides

Cover almost every European country, east and west, plus major cities.
Do have a US slant and provide much that would be of interest for the
better-heeled traveller.

Frommer's Guides

Similar in coverage and style to the Fodor's Guides.

Rough Guides

Cover most European countries, and some regions, though not
individual cities. Very good for the budget traveller but as many of
them are quite thick/heavy better to read before you go rather than
carry them with you!

Lonely Planet

Again, very good for the budget traveller but do not cover every
country and region. Good coverage of Scandinavia and Eastern
Europe.

Berlitz Pocket Guides

Very compact guides. Good for giving you a 'taster' of each country
allowing you to decide if it is worth a visit, but are short and therefore
not very detailed.

PHRASE BOOKS

More Women Travel: A Rough Guide Special (Rough Guides, 1995).
How to Find Temporary Work Abroad, Nick Vandome (How To Books,
1994).

How to Get a Job in Hotels and Catering, Mark Hempshell (How To Books, 1995).

How to Get a Job in Travel and Tourism, Mark Hempshell (How To Books, 1996).

How to Get Work on Luxury Yachts and Superyachts (Harp Publications, 1994).

How to Master Languages, Roger Jones (How To Books, 1993).

How to Spend a Year Abroad, Nick Vandome (How To Books, 1995).

International Travel Health Guide, Stuart R. Rose (Travel Medicine, 1995).

New Rail Map of Europe (Thomas Cook, 1996).

Nothing Ventured, Alison Walsh (ed.) (Harrap Columbus: Pengiun, 1991).

Thomas Cook Guide to European Night Trains (Thomas Cook, 1995).

Travellers' Health: How to Stay Healthy Abroad (Oxford University Press, 1992).

Western Europe on a Shoestring (Lonely Planet, 1995).

Working Holidays Abroad, Mark Hempshell (Kuperard, 1996).

Try the following phrasebooks. Because they're small and cover several languages in one book they won't take up much space in your backpack:

Lonely Planet: Language Survival Kits

Western Europe: Basque, Catalan, Dutch, French, German, Irish, Portuguese, Spanish.

Eastern Europe: Bulgarian, Czech, Hungarian, Romanian, Slovak.

Mediterranean Europe: Albanian, Greek, Italian, Macedonian, Maltese, Serb, Croat, Slovene.

Scandinavian Europe: Danish, Finnish, Icelandic, Norwegian, Swedish.

Other books

Thomas Cook Airports Guide: Europe (Thomas Cook, 1993).

Let's Go Eastern Europe (Macmillan, 1996). Other titles in this series cover individual European countries.

Cheap Eats Guide to Europe (Harper Collins, 1995).

Cheap Sleep Guide to Europe (Harper Collins, 1996).

Europe: The Rough Guide (Rough Guides, 1994).

Get Up and Go: Travel Survival Kit for Women, A. McCarthy (Attic Press, 1992).

Good Health for Travellers (Medicript, 1993).

Handbook for Women Travellers, G. Moss and M. Moss (Parkers Books, 1995).

Hitchhikers Guide to Europe (Harper Collins).
Hostelling International (IYHA, 1995).

FOREIGN NEWSPAPERS

Local language newspapers

Austria:
Die Press, Der Standard, Wiener Zeiting, Neue Tiroler Zeitung, Tiroler Tageszeitung, Salzburger Volkszeitung.

Belgium:
Le Soir, Antwerpse Morgan, La Meusse, Belgique No.1, L'Echo.

Denmark:
Politiken, Ekstra Bladet, Den Bla Auis, Belingske Tidende, Det Fri Aktuelt, Fryens Stifstidente, Veskysten.

Finland:
Turun Sanomat, Aamulehti, Helsingin Sanomat.

France:
Le Monde, Le Figaro, France-Soir, Sud-Ouest (Bordeaux), *La Voix* (Lille), *Ouest-France* (Rennes), *Le Progrés* (Lyon), *La Provençal* and *La Meridional* (Marseille).

Germany:
Frankfurter Allegemeine Zeitung, Die Welt, Süddeutsche Zeitung, Bayernkurier, Kölnsiche Rundschau, Weser Kurier, Stuttgarter Zeitung, Berliner Morgenpost.

Ireland:
The Irish Independent, The Irish Times, The Irish Press.

Italy:
Il Messaggero, Corriere della Sera, La Repubblica, La Voce Repubblicana (Rome), *La Nazione* (Florence), *Corriere della Sera, Il Giornale* (Milan), *La Stampa* (Turin), *Il Giornale di Napoli* (Naples), *Il Gazzetino* (Venice).

Luxembourg:
Letzeburger Journal, Luxemburger Wort.

Netherlands:
De Telegraff, De Volkskrant, Het Parool (Amsterdam), *Haagsche Courant* (The Hague), *Utrechts Nieuwsblad* (Utrecht).

Norway:
Dagbladet, Aftenposten, Arbeiderbladet.

Portugal:
Correio de Manha, O Diario, Diario (Lisbon), *Jornal de Noticias* (Oporto).

Spain:
El Pais, Diario 16, El Diario de la Costa del Sol, El Correo de Andalucia.

Sweden:
Svenska Dagbladet, Dagen, Expressen, Dagnes Nyheter, Göteborg Posten.

Switzerland:
Neue Zuricher Zeitung, Basler Zeitung, Baslerstab, Berner Zeitung, Berner Tagwacht (German), *Le Suisse, La Tribune de Genève, Journal de Genève* (French).

United Kingdom:
Daily Express, Daily Mail, Daily Mirror, Sun, Times, Guardian, Independent, London Evening Standard (London only).

English language newspapers in Europe

Belgium:
The Bulletin
Baltic States:
    Estonia: *The Baltic Independent.*
    Latvia: *The Baltic Observer.*
    Lithuania: *Baltic News, Lithuanian Weekly.*

Bulgaria:
Bulgaria News.

Greece:
Athens News, Greece Today.

Hungary:
Hungarian Week, Daily News.

Italy:
Daily American.

Portugal:
Anglo-Portuguese News.

Russia:
Moscow Times, Moscow News.

Index

SPENDING A YEAR ABROAD
Taking time out from study or work

Nick Vandome

A year abroad is now a very popular option among thousands of school leavers, students, and people taking a mid-life break. This book sets out the numerous options available from making the decision to go, to working on a kibbutz, to teaching English as a foreign language, to adapting to life at home on your return. 'Should be required reading ... Unlike most reference books this is one which should be read right through, and that is a pleasure as well as being very informative. It is totally comprehensive ... very good value for money.' *The School Librarian.* 'Excellent.' *Careers Guidance Today.* Nick Vandome is a young freelance writer who has spent a year abroad on three occasions, in France, Australia, Africa and Asia. His articles have appeared in *The Guardian, The Scotsman, The Daily Telegraph,* and elsewhere.

176pp. illus. 1 85703 459 7. 3rd edition.

HOW TO STUDY ABROAD
Your guide to successful planning and decision making

Teresa Tinsley

Studying abroad can open up a whole new horizon of opportunities, but what courses are available? How does one qualify? What does it cost? Can anyone do it? Now in a fully updated third edition, this book brings together a wealth of fascinating advice and reference information. It covers what to study (everything from short study visits to postgraduate opportunities), getting a place, entrance requirements, when and how to apply, grants and scholarships, helpful agencies and contacts, validation of courses, what to expect (teaching, services), financing your stay, accommodation, fitting in, travel and visas, health and insurance and more, and complete with a country-by-country guide. 'The book is straightforward to use, with a good index, lists of all the main reference sources likely to be found in a careers library, and is just the thing to provide a quick answer to those difficult questions.' *Phoenix/Association of Graduate Careers Advisory Services.* Teresa Tinsley BA DipEd MIL is Conferences Organiser at CILT, the Centre for Information on Language Teaching.

176pp. illus. 1 85703 169 5. 3rd edition.

HOW TO GET A JOB IN EUROPE
A guide to employment opportunities and contacts

Mark Hempshell

Europe's rise as the world's leading economic unit has made it *the* place to get a job. This book sets out exactly what opportunities exist in Europe. It will be an absolutely essential starting point for everyone job-hunting in Europe, whether as a school or college leaver, graduate trainee, technician or professional – and indeed anyone wanting to live and work as a European whether for just a summer vacation or on a more permanent basis. 'A very useful book ... a valuable addition to any careers library – well written clear and interesting.' *Phoenix/Association of Graduate Careers Advisory Services.* 'I learned a lot from the book and was impressed at the amount of information that it contained.' *Newscheck/Careers Service Bulletin.* Mark Hempshell is a freelance writer who specialises on overseas employment topics.

208pp. illus. 1 85703 177 6. 3rd edition.

HOW TO TRAVEL ROUND THE WORLD
Your practical guide to the experience of a lifetime

Nick Vandome

Fed up with the situation back home? Want to have some fun, adventure and excitement? Then this is the book for you. Written by a travel writer with extensive first-hand knowledge, this book explains how to prepare for a real globetrotting adventure, how to plan your itinerary, how to organise passports, visa permits and other international paperwork, how to plan your means of travel, kitting yourself out, planning for health and safety on the move, learning to live with different languages and cultures, earning as you go, trouble shooting, and more. The book is complete with a gazetteer of international travel information, case studies, contacts for travel, health and work, further reading, and index. Go for it – and give yourself the experience of a lifetime.

224pp. illus. 1 85703 121 0.

How To Books provide practical help on a large range of topics. They are available through all good bookshops or can be ordered direct from the distributors. Just tick the titles you want and complete the form on the following page.

___ Apply to an Industrial Tribunal (£7.99)
___ Applying for a Job (£7.99)
___ Applying for a United States Visa (£15.99)
___ Be a Freelance Journalist (£8.99)
___ Be a Freelance Secretary (£8.99)
___ Be a Local Councillor (£8.99)
___ Be an Effective School Governor (£9.99)
___ Become a Freelance Sales Agent (£9.99)
___ Become an Au Pair (£8.99)
___ Buy & Run a Shop (£8.99)
___ Buy & Run a Small Hotel (£8.99)
___ Cash from your Computer (£9.99)
___ Career Planning for Women (£8.99)
___ Choosing a Nursing Home (£8.99)
___ Claim State Benefits (£9.99)
___ Communicate at Work (£7.99)
___ Conduct Staff Appraisals (£7.99)
___ Conducting Effective Interviews (£8.99)
___ Copyright & Law for Writers (£8.99)
___ Counsel People at Work (£7.99)
___ Creating a Twist in the Tale (£8.99)
___ Creative Writing (£9.99)
___ Critical Thinking for Students (£8.99)
___ Do Voluntary Work Abroad (£8.99)
___ Do Your Own Advertising (£8.99)
___ Do Your Own PR (£8.99)
___ Doing Business Abroad (£9.99)
___ Emigrate (£9.99)
___ Employ & Manage Staff (£8.99)
___ Find Temporary Work Abroad (£8.99)
___ Finding a Job in Canada (£9.99)
___ Finding a Job in Computers (£8.99)
___ Finding a Job in New Zealand (£9.99)
___ Finding a Job with a Future (£8.99)
___ Finding Work Overseas (£9.99)
___ Freelance DJ-ing (£8.99)
___ Get a Job Abroad (£10.99)
___ Get a Job in America (£9.99)
___ Get a Job in Australia (£9.99)
___ Get a Job in Europe (£9.99)
___ Get a Job in France (£9.99)
___ Get a Job in Germany (£9.99)
___ Get a Job in Hotels and Catering (£8.99)
___ Get a Job in Travel & Tourism (£8.99)
___ Get into Films & TV (£8.99)
___ Get into Radio (£8.99)
___ Get That Job (£6.99)
___ Getting your First Job (£8.99)
___ Going to University (£8.99)
___ Helping your Child to Read (£8.99)
___ Investing in People (£8.99)
___ Invest in Stocks & Shares (£8.99)

___ Keep Business Accounts (£7.99)
___ Know Your Rights at Work (£8.99)
___ Know Your Rights: Teachers (£6.99)
___ Live & Work in America (£9.99)
___ Live & Work in Australia (£12.99)
___ Live & Work in Germany (£9.99)
___ Live & Work in Greece (£9.99)
___ Live & Work in Italy (£8.99)
___ Live & Work in New Zealand (£9.99)
___ Live & Work in Portugal (£9.99)
___ Live & Work in Spain (£7.99)
___ Live & Work in the Gulf (£9.99)
___ Living & Working in Britain (£8.99)
___ Living & Working in China (£9.99)
___ Living & Working in Hong Kong (£10.99)
___ Living & Working in Israel (£10.99)
___ Living & Working in Japan (£8.99)
___ Living & Working in Saudi Arabia (£12.99)
___ Living & Working in the Netherlands (£9.99)
___ Lose Weight & Keep Fit (£6.99)
___ Make a Wedding Speech (£7.99)
___ Making a Complaint (£8.99)
___ Manage a Sales Team (£8.99)
___ Manage an Office (£8.99)
___ Manage Computers at Work (£8.99)
___ Manage People at Work (£8.99)
___ Manage Your Career (£8.99)
___ Managing Budgets & Cash Flows (£9.99)
___ Managing Meetings (£8.99)
___ Managing Your Personal Finances (£8.99)
___ Market Yourself (£8.99)
___ Master Book-Keeping (£8.99)
___ Mastering Business English (£8.99)
___ Master GCSE Accounts (£8.99)
___ Master Languages (£8.99)
___ Master Public Speaking (£8.99)
___ Obtaining Visas & Work Permits (£9.99)
___ Organising Effective Training (£9.99)
___ Pass Exams Without Anxiety (£7.99)
___ Pass That Interview (£6.99)
___ Plan a Wedding (£7.99)
___ Prepare a Business Plan (£8.99)
___ Publish a Book (£9.99)
___ Publish a Newsletter (£9.99)
___ Raise Funds & Sponsorship (£7.99)
___ Rent & Buy Property in France (£9.99)
___ Rent & Buy Property in Italy (£9.99)
___ Retire Abroad (£8.99)
___ Return to Work (£7.99)
___ Run a Local Campaign (£6.99)
___ Run a Voluntary Group (£8.99)
___ Sell Your Business (£9.99)

How To Books

___ Selling into Japan (£14.99)	___ Use the Internet (£9.99)
___ Setting up Home in Florida (£9.99)	___ Winning Consumer Competitions (£8.99)
___ Spend a Year Abroad (£8.99)	___ Winning Presentations (£8.99)
___ Start a Business from Home (£7.99)	___ Work from Home (£8.99)
___ Start a New Career (£6.99)	___ Work in an Office (£7.99)
___ Starting to Manage (£8.99)	___ Work in Retail (£8.99)
___ Starting to Write (£8.99)	___ Work with Dogs (£8.99)
___ Start Word Processing (£8.99)	___ Working Abroad (£14.99)
___ Start Your Own Business (£8.99)	___ Working as a Holiday Rep (£9.99)
___ Study Abroad (£8.99)	___ Working in Japan (£10.99)
___ Study & Learn (£7.99)	___ Working in Photography (£8.99)
___ Study & Live in Britain (£7.99)	___ Working in the Gulf (£10.99)
___ Studying at University (£8.99)	___ Working on Contract Worldwide (£9.99)
___ Studying for a Degree (£8.99)	___ Working on Cruise Ships (£9.99)
___ Successful Grandparenting (£8.99)	___ Write a CV that Works (£7.99)
___ Successful Mail Order Marketing (£9.99)	___ Write a Press Release (£9.99)
___ Successful Single Parenting (£8.99)	___ Write a Report (£8.99)
___ Survive at College (£4.99)	___ Write an Assignment (£8.99)
___ Survive Divorce (£8.99)	___ Write an Essay (£7.99)
___ Surviving Redundancy (£8.99)	___ Write & Sell Computer Software (£9.99)
___ Take Care of Your Heart (£5.99)	___ Write Business Letters (£8.99)
___ Taking in Students (£8.99)	___ Write for Publication (£8.99)
___ Taking on Staff (£8.99)	___ Write for Television (£8.99)
___ Taking Your A-Levels (£8.99)	___ Write Your Dissertation (£8.99)
___ Teach Abroad (£8.99)	___ Writing a Non Fiction Book (£8.99)
___ Teach Adults (£8.99)	___ Writing & Selling a Novel (£8.99)
___ Teaching Someone to Drive (£8.99)	___ Writing & Selling Short Stories (£8.99)
___ Travel Round the World (£8.99)	___ Writing Reviews (£8.99)
___ Use a Library (£6.99)	___ Your Own Business in Europe (£12.99)

To: Plymbridge Distributors Ltd, Plymbridge House, Estover Road, Plymouth PL6 7PZ.
Customer Services Tel: (01752) 202301. Fax: (01752) 202331.

Please send me copies of the titles I have indicated. Please add postage & packing (UK £1, Europe including Eire, £2, World £3 airmail).

☐ I enclose cheque/PO payable to Plymbridge Distributors Ltd for £ [   ]

☐ Please charge to my ☐ MasterCard, ☐ Visa, ☐AMEX card.

Account No. [   ]

Card Expiry Date [   ] 19 ☎ **Credit Card orders may be faxed or phoned.**

Customer Name (CAPITALS) ....

Address ....

.... Postcode...............

Telephone........................... Signature ....

Every effort will be made to despatch your copy as soon as possible but to avoid possible disappointment please allow up to 21 days for despatch time (42 days if overseas). Prices and availability are subject to change without notice.

[Code BPA]